REDESIGNING THE WAY WORK WORKS

STRONG OPINION AND ADVICE
FROM 40 YEARS IN THE BUSINESS

BRUCE MORTON

DEDICATION

For my Mum and Dad:
Thanks for making me who I am and inspiring
me to be my best self every day

**For Kate and our children; Charlotte, Gwynne,
Phoebe, Curtis, Claire and Sebastien:**
Thanks for allowing me to travel the miles and work
the hours and for all of the sacrifices you make so I
can live my passions and achieve my life goals

CONTENTS

Part Three
GET READY!

Tactical Action for Strategic Value

INTRODUCTION

I learned at an early age that flexibility and a dogged work ethic are not mutually exclusive. In fact, they are effective partners in getting ahead in the business world. To see how this works, let's consider the game of golf. Enthusiasts liken the need to practice golf regularly to mastering a second language—you have to use it or lose it. So, we golfers hit the driving range, we practice our form, we return to the links often enough to commit the basic moves to muscle memory.

And yet, putting and driving are but building blocks of the game. Every fall of the ball is different. Every hazard must be newly apprised in real time. Keeping an open and agile mind is truly the key to a great game. Being from the British Isles, I love to play golf (pretty badly). But I never thought this passion would set me on my permanent career path. An adverse circumstance on the links, in hindsight, was a happy accident that showed me how to pair the mechanical aspects of work with the flexibility needed to excel.

I inherited my work ethic from my father, Maurice, and my mother, Doreen. When I was growing up, Dad was a very successful sales representative, back in the day when cold calling literally meant knocking on someone's door. Mum was a postwoman who braved rain, sleet, and snow to deliver the mail. She also found time to raise four children while keeping a weather eye on the community. Not only did she do her postal duty, she knew everybody whom she served, as well as the details of their lives gleaned from conversation and from the clues contained in postmarks, penmanship, and the timing of letters sent and received. The neighborhood joke went that Mrs. Morton knew who was pregnant before the mother did. In all seriousness, though, Mum and Dad understood that people look for purpose in their work.

It's no surprise, then, that as a lad I was up before the sun, stuffing folded newspapers into canvas bags, bound for home delivery before school each day. I'd pedal my bicycle through the streets, a bulging sack slung across each shoulder for ballast, fulfilling my paper route to make some spending money. Back then, print newspapers were full of news, gossip, and adverts. My bundles weighed a bloody ton. I got so beefed up from a few years of this toil that by the time I reached age eleven, my mother suggested I apply for a shop job with the local butcher. I did. And I adored the work.

Back then, the community meat cutter had much in common with letter carriers and sales reps. Duty was served in the form of upselling chops, roasts, and lesser cuts of meat, while the area's social scene played out inside the storefront every day. This suited me to a T. It also honed my basic business skills, while exercising the kind of flexibility needed to cater to people of different means—and to be circumspect in doling out the local intelligence. This had to do with knowing your audience. I remember my first-ever lesson in sales, along those lines, from the shop owner. He said, "Bruce, when someone asks you whether our delicious, house-made burgers have lots of onions in them, you say, 'Do you like onions?' Then, dependent on their response, you choose yours." I am sure you can guess which response I gave to each yes or no answer.

I stayed with this vocation when I left school at sixteen, wanting nothing more than to open my own shop. At the age of twenty-one, backed by my employer, I had the opportunity to do just that and bought a shop in Bourneville, the home of Cadbury's Chocolate. The proudest day of my life, up to that point, was when I replaced the sign above the shop with: BRUCE MORTON, FAMILY BUTCHER. I thought I had my work cut out for me to build a lifetime business. But that course would hold for just eight months. One day while playing golf with friends, I made a move that would change everything.

Of course, I'll never forget it. I was on hole number three. I putted to make par (a rarity), bent down to pick the ball out of the hole—and dropped to the green amid searing pain. My back had broken. Three vertebrae had snapped, rendering me motionless. I would spend ten weeks in hospital, paralyzed from the waist down, wondering if I would ever again walk, let alone work or play golf. This was no fateful accident. It turned out that I'd been born with spina bifida occulta, a birth defect in which parts of the spine do not fully close, leaving small fissures in the affected vertebrae. This form of the condition is usually mild and without symptoms, as mine was. I didn't know I had it until the vertebrae ruptured.

It took twelve months to regain my mobility and learn to walk again. But my days of lifting sides of beef were over. With no other choice, I sold the shop and approached a few staffing companies to find a job in sales. The third one I approached hired me to work for them in industrial staffing. There, I found a home for my blend of hard work and flexibility—just what was needed to bring the right workers to the right seats in the right companies. I've been in this great industry ever since.

Organizational Readiness

Surprises can be great, but not in business and critical areas of life. So, what do you do before you do something? You prepare. Even if it's choosing whether to swerve or give a dirty look to a driver who cuts you off in traffic, a preparation step comes first. Your brain recognizes the need to act. It makes a split-second choice and releases a hormone that tells muscles to tense; the muscles respond ... and—if you've made the sober choice—your hands turn the wheel sideways. The same formula holds true for any business action. Sensing a shift in the marketplace, business leaders acknowledge a concern, enter into decision-making, and set a new course. This skill is now more important than ever; I call it organizational readiness.

Now, suppose predictions indicate a seismic shift—one that can make or break your company's viability. Would you deny it and continue operations as usual? Take a small step and wait to see what happens? Maybe. If you want to be left in the dust. When expecting the equivalent of a major earthquake, leaders in any corporation would make commensurate preparations. This is where you should be in regard to your human resources and procurement protocols. That rumbling sound you hear? The ground is shifting *right now* under how we get work done and how we source, hire, and engage talent.

What are you going to do about it?

Instead of denial or a knee-jerk reaction, forward-thinking leaders want to prepare. As the great Inspector Clouseau once said (in a bad French accent), "Gather *ze* facts, examine *ze* clues, and before you know it, *ze* case will be sol-ved." If he were facing today's talent landscape, he'd be sure to put in some extra preparatory effort.

Yes, the issue is pressing, and change is upon us. But taking the time it takes to get ready will help you gain the most from this phenomenon. If your organization is not currently set up to provide a wide-ranging talent platform—that is, to meet and greet workers on their terms,from every level of availability, to engage them to achieve your goals—you're already late to the party.

But the solution is within reach, if you're ready *to become ready.* With the facts in mind about recent trends and the clues about what's to come, you'll be positioned to *do*—to embrace the new world of work and talent opportunities—and to do it right. As you read, hopefully you'll gain the awareness and the tools to customize a plan for your company.

But this book is not your "traditional" business book. I have purposely not included a boatload of blue-chip company case studies and examples that won't translate to every situation. Instead, I include material based on the pattern of successes and failures I've seen around the world in the last forty years, all preparing us for this moment. What you are about to read comes from my personal observation and informed opinion, with a little help from my in-the-know friends.

As with all free advice (or for the nominal price of a book), you can take or leave this information—but you have much to gain from reading with an open mind and trying out a few suggestions. I am confident you will be glad you did. At the very least, your business will become more prepared and agile than it was last week. And last week's long gone! I've written this book to discuss *how to prepare*—to effectively send yourself back in time to meet the future. And then to catapult forward.

The Gathering Storm

Old thinking typically stands in the way of progress and innovation. *It worked yesterday, so it'll work tomorrow.* This may have been true for hiring, once, but no more. It's not just that the traditional talent pool has shrunk in many areas of the world, though it surely has. More significantly, the habits and desires of those in the pool have evolved. So, sticking with the old ways may cause those fish to swim elsewhere.

What's needed today is a platform from which to cast for the right people, and a nurturing work stream to which they can contribute their gifts, swim away when it suits them, and to which they can return when the time is right. But human resources are only part of the equation. In order to optimize the talent that you've landed, the work design must match your operational objectives, and vice versa. So, we're talking about striking a balance between two very dynamic entities. We're talking about a new kind of strategy.

Many business leaders are well versed in one realm or the other— either human resource management or decision-making around workflows and organizational goals. In the future, the one we're already living in, both skills are equally critical. To hone them, there are several avenues we can take and several tools at our disposal. Standing between the average executive and those solutions is *history*. We must understand how we got to this point, in order to make the most effective, informed moves.

I've been at both ends of the spectrum myself. As head of innovation for Allegis Global Solutions, a global workforce management solutions firm, I felt the shift before I truly understood what was happening. When we realized that the status quo had left the docking station, my team took a deep dive into the past trends that led to present hiring and performance circumstances. Then, based on the promise of unfolding technology, we projected where the current wave would take us. From that big picture, we developed what we call **QuantumWork**, a strategy and technology that minimizes the barriers in hiring full-time, contract, freelance, and other types of workers in order to best meet well-defined business needs. Our vision is to provide universal access to all forms of talent and to seamlessly achieve all operational goals and business objectives ... to be relevant through change by deconstructing work to its constituent parts and following the workforce wherever it may go ... to optimize cost, speed, and human and machine skill. In short, the goal is to make companies as agile as they can be at any moment in time.

I now, aptly, head up strategy for Allegis Global Solutions and speak often to groups concerned with marketplace success, and the people and work design that help achieve it. This whole paradigm echoes my own work history. It's what has brought me full-circle to the insights in this book. Executives carry much more than reasoning and an affinity for market movements to the table. We bring our previous life experiences to bear when faced with big issues, of which today's changing talent landscape is easily one of the most important. Change is here, and it will affect every single business on the planet.

Riding the Wave

I learnt firsthand that adversity is a terrific driver of innovation. But the majority of people don't like change. So, we often remain paired with the status quo until it is no longer sustainable. Like a butcher's sudden inability to hoist slabs of meat, the disappearance of a centralized workforce is handicapping today's businesses that are stuck in yesterday. And any corporation laboring under a handicap will not survive. Those that are slow to change course cannot keep up with the pace of technology, the market, and even customers' and workers' attention spans. These all move at light speed now and show no signs of slowing.

How flexible is your company? How ready is it to leap the hurdles toward the incredible opportunities that lie on the other side? Because that is what the new talent landscape promises businesses that are both prepared and agile. You are now poised to begin the most important conversation in which your organization will ever engage. For acquiring the best talent is no longer a simple equation that is static and that will work for everybody. Hiring to get the work done will entail an ongoing debate, a discussion that brings together all the parties—HR, Procurement, and the entire C-suite; line managers, employees, contractors, freelancers; corporate teams, crowdsourcing collectives, and everything in between.

I once thought I'd happily be a butcher for life, until events broke down the walls in my thinking. The event that made me grateful to walk gave me a different outlook, one in which the glass is not only half full, but potentially bottomless—even my golf game has improved the last couple of years! This is where you and I stand today in understanding the best way to get work done, in appealing to all forms of talent, and in purposefully overachieving our objectives to move our companies forward. There can be much pain, or there can be great promise.

Let's talk about it.

Part One

ARE YOU READY?

The Future Is Now

CHAPTER 1

The Shifting Balance between Work and Workers

What makes "work" work for us? Is it people? Products? Great management? In any given market sector, all things being equal, the organizations that find an edge win the lion's share. Often, a kind of divine intuition is involved—a finger on the pulse of consumer demand, or economic trends, or breakthrough technology that allows companies to act ahead of their competitors. With information available instantly via the internet and with marketplace dynamics shifting into overdrive, though, it's difficult to make any move these days before someone else has. But there is one source of leverage that every business can tap. It doesn't exist "out there." The answers lie within.

How many of us consider new ways of leveraging the raw materials that exist inside our own organizations? The knowledge and expertise of internal employees and contract workers, whose intellect or craftsmanship create items of value bound for market, are—or were—considered the bulk of these proprietary resources. Until recently, the best way to make the most of them was to: a) hire the best people;

b) keep them there; and c) encourage innovation. But even those actions had limitations. Attracting and selecting the best depended upon geographic and budget availability. Retention was and is an inexact science at best. And innovation required a complicated blend of the right people, the right timing, and good fortune. Now, however, prerequisites and our understanding of productivity have changed.

To achieve the state of organizational readiness that allows companies to surge past the competition, we must put work processes on par with talent management. We must make decisions on whom we hire *based on the macro and micro objectives we face.* We must deconstruct the work so that we can reconstruct a partnership between what must be done, who can best do it, and how. This is the new frontier to be mapped out in order to stay even with, let alone a step ahead of, the crowd. In fact, companies that are already doing this *are* leaders in their fields. This new approach must be defined and refined before we can ask people to get to work on it.

Meet the Stars of Our Show:
The Work Design Architect and the "Talentsumer"

Here are two big players that you're going to hear a lot more about ...

Work Design Architect

This is a designated person who understands, designs, and gives strategic advice on the best way to get work done. The role requires the ability to deeply comprehend an organization's business objectives and turn those goals into a structured

---

workforce architecture and framework. **A work design architect:**

- Partners across the business to deconstruct "old-fashioned" job descriptions and help leaders rethink tasks and outputs
- Defines the context of all roles in the company's success
- Designs processes that give workers a consumer-like experience
- Understands which tasks can and should be automated, and partners with RPA (robotic process automation) and AI (artificial intelligence) groups to get that done
- Analyzes performance metrics to design new ways of working
- Uses a hearts-and-minds approach to change traditional mindsets

Obvious synergies exist between this role and that of a design architect in the construction industry. For physical structures, design architects analyze sites and create plans for construction, remodeling, additions, and/or repairs. They attend to the style of the finished project while meeting all building requirements and codes. An even better construction analogy is that of quantity surveyors. They take the blueprint drawing of a house and calculate which resources and materials are needed to build the structure, as well as lay out the order in which everything should be built. They create a critical path analysis and time frame for each stage of a project, plus a cost/

time/quality-versus-risk profile. A **work design architect** does exactly that by taking the business objectives as the blueprint and designing the best way to get the work done!

The "Talentsumer"

A generational shift in the workforce and changing conditions have produced workers with different values, desires, and expectations than their predecessors. Today's **Talentsumers** came of age in a consumer-friendly atmosphere, in which they grew to expect and insist on responsiveness to their needs. These job candidates, employees, contractors, and freelancers may have enjoyed more flexibility and open communication from their parents than earlier generations, and so they project these desires on the employer who might engage a majority of their time.

Because workers today face shorter tenures, less job stability, higher expectations, expenses, and potentially longer lives than those who came before them, they have a list of urgent demands. **Talentsumers** prefer to work for employers who meet their need to:

- build skills and expand the types of work they can take on
- work on projects with a start and end—not BAU
- receive frequent feedback and coaching from inspiring leaders

> - get continuous training, development and visible paths toward promotion
> - enjoy a flexible hiring status and work hours
>
> As workers in other age groups have seen the benefits of these conditions, they, of course, want them too. So, gradually, the key people that employers pursue have become **Talentsumers**. We want ways to enrich our lives, and in return, we contribute to the task at hand, the overall culture, and the company's success. Everyone wins!

In this context, the leverage every organization seeks is about intelligently optimizing talent in light of our business needs. As we shall see, new ways of sourcing great workers smash geographic and even budget boundaries. Despite current restrictions, you *can* get the people you need. But *their* needs are changing. In order to optimize the value they bring to your organization, you must first understand their *why*—and then enable, encourage, motivate, and reward them to do their very best work with you. If you don't, your competitors will.

I've begun this discussion with you to convey the seriousness of the moment. And this is not just based on the latest white papers I've read, although you'll find many referenced in this book. I bring forty years of observation to the topic, as seen from my wide-angle perch, thirty thousand feet in the air, crisscrossing the globe to consult with business leaders about

... this state of organizational readiness should be our goal.

how best to use their people power. I've seen the range of corporate energy run from stagnant to off the charts when change is made for the better. I can definitively say that organizations capitalize on what is done best and boldly innovate when they marry work design with talent optimization. You may disagree, and that's fine. But I would argue, you owe it to your business to at least join the conversation. I have included some credited anecdotes throughout this book, that will hopefully hammer home some of the more salient points.

While myriad factors affect the way work gets done and shape our methods for attracting, motivating, and retaining talent, I've identified three key drivers that I expect will become prominent over the months and years to come:

- Rise of the "Talentsumer"
- Rise of digital workers
- Talent integration

My former business partner, Emma Reynolds, and I coined the term "Talentsumer" some years ago—when we founded our workforce design consultancy, e3. The label describes the growing trend in workers acting more like consumers than employees in the workplace, largely pushed by changing generational perspectives. The demands of these workers have increased to match their priorities. Here is what HR and Procurement departments face: *this workforce segment will meet the surge in digital help and intelligent automation, made possible by robotics and artificial intelligence technology, head on.* Newly appreciated sources of talent that include contractors, freelancers, and communities of workers will need to be integrated with traditional internal employees, and the whole process of attracting and acquiring them must be centralized and streamlined. We'll talk about how employers should respond to these trends in Chapters 2 and 3.

These are the things that company leaders must take into account as the balance between work and workers shifts. The three issues affecting our talent pools—**Talentsumers' demands, new opportunities in employing digital workers, and total talent integration**—form the touch points for most of this book. Understanding and adapting to them will help us better manage what it is that we actually do and how we do it. And it is this state of organizational readiness that should be our goal. I believe, when combined with optimized human resources, this formula will help companies survive. Those that master it will excel.

The Answers Are Within

While running a workshop for a financial services company in the UK, I asked the engagement question, *How easy do we make it for you to do great work?* A twenty-year-old marketing assistant answered by bringing up a questionable process. He wondered why the company paid £25 for a credit-check report on every new enquiry when they all seemed to pass. He was too circumspect to say that this seemed like a waste of time and money.

When I met with that firm's executive board, I relayed the question to the CFO. His response? "Because we've always done it." After a long, embarrassing silence, the CEO asked, "Uhm, what percentage of credit scores pass?" Nobody knew, so I said (somewhat smugly, but desperately trying not to show it that most of them passed: "In the last twelve months, you've paid for sixty-four thousand checks. Less than 5 percent of them fail—which, by the way, could have been identified in-house at a further stage."

The decision was made right then not to conduct that check until much later in the process, with only the enquiries that were at sale point (approximately six thousand would get that far.) So, the company reduced their credit-check cost from £1.6m to £150k—a savings of £1,450,000 that went straight to the bottom line. The happy postscript to that story? The young lad got a promotion to supervisor, and his annual salary rose from £20,000 to £25,000.

I consider this sort of perpetual flexibility and openness to listen to your people and change, critical to success in the new landscape. It requires a deep grasp of what it takes to transact work in a given business, plus the agility to link market conditions with internal processes and a real-world knowledge of the talent we have on hand. How great a change must we make? Let's look at the old model and where I believe we'll need to be in the immediate future—like, now. The gap between them is the distance we must leap.

Point A: The Old Norms

Remember when you were a child and one or both of your parents got ready for work? They put on the appropriate clothing, kissed you goodbye, and went off to the office, storefront, factory, or farm. Their commute was short or long, but it took them away from home to the site where they generated their paychecks. That was then.

Drawing people together made it easy to supervise and motivate them en masse. Workers could see their peers laboring and compare each other's performance. If someone were disciplined or rewarded, the action had a trickle-down effect on the rest of the staff. It made the group loyal to their employer, whether by carrot or stick. They could witness their elders enjoying stable employment and exiting the company after many decades, generally with some sort of nest egg, and expect to do the same.

This structure allowed employers to attract and acquire talent fairly simply. Everyone knew what the definition of work was: typically, eight hours daily, performing a proscribed set of tasks. This job description did not change much; emerging business opportunities usually entailed creating new positions rather than enhancing or expanding old ones. If times got tough and workers had to be let go, those who remained picked up the unfulfilled tasks, usually without additional remuneration. They knew they were "lucky to have a job" and so they quietly soldiered on.

That world of work remained largely the same from the eighteenth- and nineteenth-century Industrial Revolution through the late twentieth century. People got hired with the expectation of some form of training to do the job, a career spread over forty years (ideally, including a couple of promotions), and a livelihood in return. They identified most closely with the entity that employed them, not the actual tasks that they performed.

I think back to my parent's generation: I grew up in the 1960s in Alvechurch, a village on the outskirts of Birmingham in the UK. There, the big employer was known as "the Austin," a vehicle-manufacturing company owned by British Leyland (since sold to Tata). Back then, if my mum and dad went to someone's house for dinner on a Saturday night, a typical conversation amongst the ladies in the kitchen might go something like this:

> Wife One: "Hello. We haven't met before. What does your husband do?"
> Wife Two: "He works down the Austin."
> Wife One: "Oh, thought so. What does he do there?"
> Wife Two: "I'm not sure. He's been there twenty-two years. I think he works in the drawing office or something."

First, imagine a woman today getting to know another woman by asking what her husband does! Notice that the company name and length of service were far more salient than the work performed, back then. Notably, it was an era when the division of labor within the home was very clear also, and the demarcation continued in the workplace. Time spent at the office or factory often led to wholesale behavioral changes in individuals whose workdays began when they arrived "at work" and ended when they left the property. They dressed differently at work, acted differently, and in some cases, even responded to another name. This was considered normal, and even desirable. There was a whole span of the 1970s when you knew you'd made it if coworkers called you by your initials alone. Remember: *Who shot J. R.?* Unfortunately, my initials are B. M.—American readers will recognize the drawback of that system for me....

So, many people in the last two generations had a persona for home (hopefully, that was the real person) and a persona adopted for work. Companies even utilized psychometric "tests" in the hiring process to help them understand the real person behind the work-mask traits.

That all started changing around the 1980s with the ascent of Yuppies, short for "young, urban (or upwardly-mobile) professionals." The long workday became a macho status symbol for both sexes, although predictably, mostly men! It went right along with stopping for a quick drink on the way home from the office, name-dropping loudly while networking at the wine bar and waving a Porsche key fob around. Yet it wasn't that far removed from earlier generations' pride of self-sacrifice, lampooned in the classic Monty Python comedic sketch, "The Four Yorkshiremen." It's hilarious. If you're a Baby Boomer, you may know it; if not you can find it on YouTube. The sketch builds to a crescendo with this boast, portrayed by Eric Idle, which eerily echoes the workaholic ethic of the 1980s and 1990s:

"I had to get up in the morning at ten o'clock at night, half an hour before I went to bed, eat a lump of cold poison, work twenty-nine hours a day down mill, and pay the mill owner for permission to come to work. And when we got home, our dad would kill us and dance about on our graves, singing, 'Hallelujah!'"

Attempting to outdo one's coworker had never been taken to such hyperbolic heights. The real trend persisted, illustrated by such cinematic characters as Gordon Gekko (Michael Douglas) in the film *Wall Street* and Jane Craig (Holly Hunter) in *Broadcast News*, both—not coincidentally—1987 productions. Eventually, however, burning the candle at both ends could no longer be topped by longer work hours. Indeed, by the end of the nineties, that kind of striving was no longer tolerated by the workers themselves. Acceptance of the rat race was giving way to a preference for work/life balance and the basic self-respect it implied. Witness 1999's film *Office Space*, in which Initech IT department friends Peter, Michael, and Samir attempt to lighten their workloads through criminal activity, even as their coworker Milton suffers further indignities.

So, by the year 2000, we had gone from acceptance of Gordon Gekko's "lunch is for wimps" to Milton's frustrated demolition of his employer's office building by fire. No more would the company provide everything workers needed to march through thirty-year careers. The concept of "keep your head down and wait for your pension" disappeared with the Walkman and Magic 8 Ball. The idea that working men and women could "do it all"—work late hours and raise a family, too—got worn out.

The old norms were going up in smoke.

Point B: The New Normal

Let's face it, that work/life balance thing never really got off the ground. Sure, some of the big investment banks attempted to help their committed male workers streamline their lives: *We'll send your laundry to the cleaners, shine your shoes at your desk, walk your dog, do your shopping*—just about anything short of *we'll sleep with your wife!* But, even if your company offered such time-saving "benefits," it was only so you'd be free to work harder, longer. Today's version of that is called work/life integration, and it was made possible over the subsequent years by emerging technology: the FAX machine (remember that thing?), the internet, the laptop, and the cell phone. This blending of "work" and "life" now lets us be more productive and work flexible hours in more casual settings. It enables our work switch to be always On, but not worn out.

Think about it. Work used to be someplace we'd GO. Now it's something we DO. If you are younger—a Millennial or Gen Z designate—this is all you've ever known; if you are a Baby Boomer, like me, or at the upper end of Generation X, you may remember when you entered this new world in which work, and life merged. It was probably early in the 2000s: It's a Sunday morning. You turn on your laptop, go and grab a coffee while the dial-up connects, and then you check your emails ... only to see a message from your boss. For a second, you think, *WTF, emailing me on a Sunday! What is he/she thinking?* Then you reply.

The first time you pressed the Send button in such circumstances was your entry into the world in which we all now live. Yes, we used to get up, get dressed, and GO to work. It seems so quaint. Now we work on our phones and laptops on the way to work, and on the way back from work. We get home, eat, put the kids to bed, and then get back online. Some of us never leave the house. In fact, these days, my guess is the majority of us never really leave work.

I'm not saying this change is all bad. Blurring the lines between home and work means we are more likely and able to be "ourselves" in the work setting. We feel free to speak up, extrapolate from our personal experience, and bring to bear knowledge and skills above our defined and expected field of expertise. Maybe things we've learned or done as a hobby or with our friends and families can shed light on a particular work issue. A personal passion might drive us to volunteer for certain professional tasks. A connection on LinkedIn or Facebook may have knowledge that we need to solve a business issue. (Remember when companies tried to ban access to LinkedIn and Facebook in the workplace? I used to say, "Good luck with that; people have phones!") These strengths, which in the old days were tamped down, add value to our contribution as employees and contractors. The ability to follow our interests or lend our mastery to a project motivates us in ways that a salary alone certainly cannot.

The change for employers, though, may be more sharply defined. If work is life and life is work, we expect more from the latter. People don't just want a job anymore. They want to contribute, feel they've made a difference, and have the chance to continually develop their skills and increase their worth. They want to be in demand, not just add to the worker supply. At the same time, they insist on the same treatment in their work lives that they get in their personal lives. And in today's society, that means being courted, respected, and rewarded—in other words, treated as a consumer.

Workers who have grown up with cutting-edge technology and an ever-increasing ability to get work done as quickly and easily as possible—Generations X, Y, and Z—also carry high expectations for doting customer service. This means that competitive organizations must rethink how the employee and contract worker experience can most closely align with the consumer experience, in order to attract and keep the best talent from these groups. It may mean making work more convenient, the way online shopping is—say, with flex time or remote options. It might mean offering ways to build skills about which individuals are enthusiastic, but may not obviously benefit the organization.

But, again, this change for employers is not all bad. It frees people from some of the outdated, old ways to which they've clung. Unleashing the brilliance of every individual allows companies to optimize their skills, imagination, and efficiency. This new paradigm will increase a company's overall productivity more significantly than any of the corporate-centric initiatives that were taken in the past.

And this only makes sense. We are living in an empowered world in which people are no longer limited to learning job-related skills at work; they probably have newer technology in their homes than many employers can provide. Now, if we can train them in new skills while they are on the clock, we are saving them time. That holds real value for them.

In the past, the access to, and the use of technology was solely work related. Today, it's societal. That's one of the things that has led to the "consumerization" of work. We have lived through a consumer revolution, and we are now experiencing a revolution in the workplace: the age of the Talentsumer. This affords individual workers more power, in some ways, than the organizations that are lucky enough to be enjoying their company for the moment!

And the moment is fleeting. I say that because worker tenure is definitely decreasing, for many reasons that we'll discuss later. The challenge to HR and management is that, because of a new temporal framework, the nature and value of retention is changing. But perhaps it is our definition of retention that also needs a makeover. A common misperception is that Gen Y or Millennial workers have no loyalty. That is simply incorrect; they are incredibly loyal—just not necessarily to the same things that their parents were. Retaining them becomes more situational.

Members of these demographic groups are now more likely to show dedication to a distinct craft or skill than to an organization. Some of this attitude may have come from seeing their parents serve decades in a company, only to have their careers ended by "downsizing," with no loyalty in play by the company. Many in these younger generations were raised indulgently, hearing that "anything is possible" and "every child is special." They may have an exaggerated sense of their individual merits, or the importance of those merits in given roles. And, for many, the parental safety net was extended much longer than in previous generations. These younger workers may have enjoyed the luxury of taking longer to decide who they wanted to be when they grew up while their helicopter parents hovered overhead. This could explain the group's preference for flex time and an interactive leadership style.

These sentiments have seeped into the general consciousness so that, these days, workers are all more likely to be loyal to a craft than a paymaster. And even the humble types have a sense of propriety— and rightly so—about their grasp on that craft. They know it has value, and they know it is in demand. Craft is to workers as dollars are to consumers. Therefore, Talentsumers expect an employer to provide the same level of "service" they get from their favorite consumer brands. And this is where loyalty and retention take on extra meaning. Just imagine having your employees and contractors feel as passionate about your company as they are about brands they respect, like Microsoft, Apple, Nike, Amazon, etc. Treat these workers like consumers, and you can get that passion and loyalty. It may come in the form of retention, referrals to other talent, or really, really great work on a single project. What we *expect* from our workers must change, so that we can get the most out of our experience with them—and they with us.

A Letter from a Millennial: shared by Lisa McLeod, Founder, McLeod & More, Inc., and Author of *Selling with Noble Purpose* (Wiley, 2012)

Attracting and keeping top Millennial talent is a burning issue for leaders. Millennials are 35 percent of the workforce. By 2020, they'll be 46 percent of the working population. Some of our most successful clients—G Adventures, Google, and Hootsuite—are filled with Millennials who are on fire for their jobs. Yet many organizations struggle to attract, and retain, top talent from that generation.

A member of our firm, Elizabeth Lotardo, is a Millennial and cum laude graduate of Boston University. She wrote this letter to share insights about what top-performing Millennials want and how leaders can ignite the "energy of a thousand suns."

An Open Letter to Management:

You hired us thinking this one might be different; this one might be in it for the long haul. We're six months in, giving everything, we have, then suddenly, we drop a bomb on you. We're quitting.

We know the stereotypes. Millennials never settle down. We're drowning in debt for useless degrees. We refuse to put our phone away. We are addicted to lattes even at the expense of our water bill. Our bosses aren't wrong about these perceptions. But, pointing out our sometimes-irresponsible spending and fear of interpersonal commitment isn't going to solve your problem. You still need us. We're the ones who've mastered social media, who have the energy of a thousand suns, and who will knock back 5-dollar macchiatos until the job is done perfectly.

I've worked in corporate America, administrative offices, advertising agencies, and restaurants. I've had bosses ranging from 24 to 64. I've had bosses I loved, and bosses I didn't. I've seen my peers quit, and I've quit a few times myself. Here's what's really behind your Millennials' resignation letter:

1. You tolerate low-performance

It's downright debilitating to a high achiever. I'm working my heart out and every time I look up Donna-Do-Nothing is contemplating how long is too long to take for lunch. I start wondering why leadership tolerates this.

Is that the standard here? No thanks.

Fact: Poor performers have a chilling effect on everyone.

2. ROI is not enough for me.

I spent Sunday thinking about how I can make a difference to our customers. Now it's Monday morning, what do I hear? Stock price. Billing. ROI. Suddenly, my Monday power playlist seems useless. I'm sitting in a conference room listening to you drag on about cash flow.

I was making more money bartending in college than I am at this entry-level job. You say I'll get a raise in a year if the company hits a certain number? So what? I need something to care about today. Talk to me about how we make a difference, not your ROI report.

Fact: Organizations with a purpose bigger than money have a growth rate triple that of their competitors.

3. Culture is more than free Panera.

Don't confuse culture with collateral. Yes, I am a cash-strapped Millennial who really appreciates free lunch. But I don't wake up at 6AM every day to play foosball in the break room. I'm not inspired to be more innovative over a Bacon Turkey Bravo.

I need to be surrounded by people who are on fire for what we're doing. I need a manager who is motivated to push boundaries and think differently. Working in a cool office is really awesome. So is free lunch. But a purposeful culture is more important.

Fact: A culture of purpose drives exponential sales growth

4. It's OK to get personal

Treat me like a number? I'll return the favor. This job will quickly become nothing more than my rent payment. I'll start living for Friday and counting down the minutes until 5. After a few months of that, I'll probably have a drunken epiphany and realize I want more out of my life than this.

Then I'll prove your assumptions right. 8 months in, I'll quit and leave. Or worse, I'll quit and stay, just like Donna-Do-Nothing.

That's not good for either of us. Here's what you need to know:

I was raised to believe I could change the world. I'm desperate for you to show me that the work we do here matters, even just a little bit. I'll make copies, I'll fetch coffee, I'll do the grunt work. But I'm not doing it to help you get a new Mercedes.

I'll give you everything I've got, but I need to know it makes a difference to something bigger than your bottom line.

Signed,

A Millennial

And yet, so many companies are still being run through hierarchies that were created to manage large volumes of workers doing menial tasks in the fields and factories of the agricultural and industrial ages. As the balance between work and workers shifts ever more rapidly, so, too, must our expectations shift. This means that what we currently call *employer brand, candidate experience,* and *employee engagement* will become even more critical considerations for every business, across all industries and markets.

These terms, of course, will eventually fall by the wayside, along with the label *"permanent" employee*. As companies realize that ethics and values are more than just buzzwords to the new generations of workers, culture becomes not just a selling point but a business imperative. As talent pools become more fluid, our expectations of who can do the work—and what our relationship with them will be—must change. In light of these factors, our business goals and processes should be constantly reevaluated. This is the stage of organizational readiness that will fuel our businesses for their journey to the future.

And this is the point we need to reach as soon as possible, if not sooner. Let's talk about how best to traverse the distance between point A and point B. It involves understanding the new talent.

CHAPTER 2

The Rise of the Free Agent, Digital Worker, and "Talentsumer"

I n terms of hiring norms, we are at a *Creature from the Black Lagoon* moment. The 1954 3-D movie presented a missing-link discovery—a fictional "gill-man" that supposedly bridged the evolution between sea and land animals. In similar fashion, out of the swamp of adversity has risen the worker that the work needs.

Besides the generational priority shift toward a consumer mentality, two more events took place in the past decade that have led us to the current talent landscape: the financial crisis of 2007–08, and the surge in digital technology. These tipping points abruptly changed the nature of the working relationship—how employers utilize and pay their workers. What began as a short-term solution to hiring freezes and shrinking bottom lines evolved into what looks like a new model with staying power. In much the same way that cash-strapped academic institutions in the previous century began relying more heavily on adjunct rather than tenured professors, many businesses were forced to look beyond permanent hires after the banking collapse. Enter the contingent worker ... and cue the robots.

The Seeds of Free Agency

Facts: the concept of a job for life is all but dead and unlikely to ever be revived. As the old expectations began to die out, workers who found themselves between jobs looked for ways to make ends meet. Stints at day labor and temporary gigs gave the otherwise unemployed a taste of a new career model. As long as staffing agencies provided such jobs, a worker could move among short-term engagements indefinitely. In the process, their network of prospective employers would continue to grow.

Next, the advent of the internet and its wider advertising net meant that those with expertise could strike out on their own. Scouring the help wanted ads on Craigslist was one source for contract work. Setting up an inexpensive website allowed contractors to hang out their shingles and let the work come to them.

Employers were slower to latch on to this way of thinking. *Outsourcing* was a dirty word in its younger years, considered an underhanded tactic employed only by the most cut-throat corporations. But, like the embrace of workaholic habits in the 1980s, hiring from outside one's own company became a badge of honor for businesses seeking leverage wherever they could find it. Then came the mortgage and banking crises. Once the economy tanked, the financial benefits of slashing traditional hiring costs could not be denied. Organizations that needed talent that they did not house themselves dipped into the contractor pool and found the water was just fine. Before you could say "adjunct professor," tenured positions in companies were cut or put on hold, and contingent workers were brought in to do what needed to be done.

Traditionally, short-term workers had helped meet seasonal or changing consumer demands. Contractors were used for finite projects with clear boundaries. It was easy for employers to slice up this short-term work and serve it to temporary hires. As that became more palatable to both parties, companies began to look more closely at their workflows to see which portions might be outsourced.

Today, contract talent represents a significant proportion of the workforce—and a growing proportion of staffing assignments. According to the U.S. Department of Labor, as of 2016, more than 30 percent of American workers were classified as "non-traditional," meaning they were not formally employed by the organizations for which they worked. These ranks are projected to reach as much as 50 percent of all those employed in the private sector before long. We're seeing a similar pattern take shape in Europe and Asia.

Now that turning to free agents is considered not only legitimate but financially prudent, a pressing question for human resources practitioners is: *who are these people?*

You will have reached out to this free-flowing talent pool already. So far, this incohesive group is like a wayward river that keeps redefining its banks. Contingent workers are most commonly:

- Temporary staffing agency employees
- Functional skilled contractors
- Interim or acting executives
- Individual freelancers
- Consultants

Emerging platforms and trends widen this pool to include:

- Staff on loan from other organizations
- Crowdsourced applicants
- Craft collectives
- Unpaid interns
- Volunteers

But it's not what you call these workers today that will matter tomorrow. *Whom you select and how you source them* are fast becoming the big questions. And how you handle those variables will have the greatest competitive impact in the immediate business future. As we will see in Chapter 3, the answers should come from the nature of the work itself. For now, let's look at one more type of staffer—one that doesn't make the human roll call.

The Option of Digital Help

In 1989, moviegoers were treated to a sneak preview of the digital age when Marty McFly (Michael J. Fox) and Doc Brown (Christopher Lloyd) jumped aboard their modified DeLorean time machine and traveled to the year 2015 in *Back to the Future Part II*. Today, director Robert Zemeckis's vision of 2015 reminds us of portents that have come to pass from another iconic motion picture, Stanley Kubrick's *2001*—such as talking computers that seem a bit too independent for our tastes. In the first *Back to the Future* sequel, Marty and Doc break the time/space barrier in their flying sports car to visit a world dominated by artificial intelligence. In the 2015 setting, work in all types of services from petrol stations to cafés are delegated to machines, not human beings.

Much of what once seemed a far-off future in both Kubrick's and Zemeckis's films has entered the here and now. While flying cars still have a ways to go, the reality encountered by Marty and Doc isn't so far removed from our own. Whether it's using a self-service grocery checkout or having a conversation with an automated phone system, we now routinely enjoy, and sometimes get annoyed with, machine-generated services that were once carried out by people. Breakthroughs in robotics, digital matrices, and machine learning have brought us to this point.

The new technology holds all sorts of promise for consumers—flying cars included—but it may be even more significant to employers in the long run. While some workers may be supplanted by machines, the changes will likely generate new work opportunities. This has been true since the dawn of the Industrial Revolution. Once considered a death knell to labor, automation made many workers' lives easier even as it prompted others to find new career paths. Fear of change, however, obscured the potential gains that mechanization might bring. These apprehensions led to sabotage, labor strikes, and violent standoffs between workers and management around the world, such as the Luddite movement in the nineteenth-century textile factories of Great Britain and the early twentieth-century woolen mills of Lawrence, Massachusetts.

We are seeing echoes of these fears as the application of AI invades certain job sectors, including manufacturing and customer service. But mechanization of those types of jobs has been underway for quite some time, and the world of work has still survived. It may fall to employers to convince the public that computers and robots enhanced by machine learning are more beneficial than detrimental. Defining the classes of existing technology might help. The digital worker of the future (which is *now,* by the way) may be driven by one or more types of "thinking":

- **Assisted intelligence** automates repetitive, standardized, or time-consuming tasks and provides information. Two examples are price scanners used in stores and GPS navigation programs. Technologies such as lasers and satellites combine with computer databases to do things like locate merchandise price figures and offer directions or road conditions to drivers.

- **Augmented intelligence** makes human and machine collaboration possible in evaluating large amounts of data and facilitating decision-making. Complex, yet efficient, interactions between digital programs and human workers enable enhanced services such as car ride-sharing businesses and in-house manufactured dental crowns.

- **Autonomous intelligence**, in which computers themselves relieve humans of organic cognitive processes, is being developed right now. Robotics advancements are enabling more complex movement, and adaptive technology shows machines how to sort information and learn from it. These next-generation machines will be able to evaluate data, make decisions, and even take action on their own. The corporate earnings previews that appear on Forbes's website, for instance, are already being generated by algorithms without human involvement. We'll see further results in things like self-driving vehicles and other innovations that are still to come.

- **Robotic process automation** is software that can be easily programmed to do basic tasks across applications, just as human workers do. It is designed to reduce human employees' burden of simple, repetitive, tasks, such as retrieving invoices from email and typing the relevant data into forms in a bookkeeping program.

So, what does this mean to business leaders and HR folks looking to build the ideal flexible team? Erik Brynjolfsson and Andrew McAfee, in their great book, *The Second Machine Age* (W. W. Norton, 2016), forecast that machines may take over as much as 50 percent of certain jobs within the next fifteen years. I believe that companies must consider this development a welcome addition to their competitive arsenal rather than a draw-down of expertise. It's just one element of organizational readiness—the agile state that businesses will need to maintain in order to quickly adapt to changing conditions, whether regarding the talent pool, supply chain, or market demands. We'll look at the broader picture of that in the next chapter.

But I cannot overstate the importance of businesses reaching a critical knowledge mass on this subject as quickly as possible. Investment trends in AI by companies such as Microsoft, Google, Apple, and Amazon mean that innovation will only come faster and more furiously. And the integration of digital workers into

The potential of AI is made apparent by the level of investment it is attracting from some of the biggest organizations in the world.

the larger employee framework will affect all businesses—those that use them, and those that don't. Professionals in HR and Procurement will find themselves hiring and managing smaller human staffs and larger digital ones.

The working people who remain will have different values, expectations, and skill sets. As old staff positions disappear and new ones replace them, competition for talented people to fill companies' needs will no doubt grow more intense, if the current global shortage of in-demand skills persists. This is why the second important element of organizational readiness—an upgrade of workflow evaluation and design—is vital. How can we know who (or what) should perform a given task if we aren't explicit about what the work entails, and which functions are needed to complete it?

In Part Two of this book, we'll talk more about how top companies are already deconstructing work and pairing it with a customized workforce. You can bet they are not shying away from using AI and RPA strategically to do superior work for which machines are suited—in a way that is most efficient and cost-effective. Businesses will always need good people. But the judicious use of AI and digital employees is one aspect of the shifting balance between workers and work that will need to be not only accepted but used to its utmost advantage.

Talentsumers Are Here to Stay

This leads us back to the human workforce. For the foreseeable future, we will likely fashion our teams from a combination of digital and human employees, on a combined contingent and "permanent" basis—or whatever permanence morphs into over time. Among the human talent pool, the majority of whom these days are now members of Generation Y, demographics and values are changing. To move with that curve, management needs a new lens through which to view these more demanding workers—and new policies that address their reality.

Before you discount the value of accommodating workers' new attitudes toward work, remember that we no longer have the luxury of an "employer's market." Even as far back as 2015, a survey of three hundred HR professionals by Human Capital Institute and Allegis Global Solutions showed that the candidate, not the employer, now holds the power in hiring negotiations.[1] The majority of respondents reported having shifted their hiring strategies, such as increasing starting salaries, due to higher turnover for key roles and a longer time to fill a greater volume of open positions. The candidate is now well and truly in the driver's seat, and we had better hand them the keys.

We'll get to how best to compete for talent in different demographic groups in later chapters. For now, let's look at what it is these prevailing Talentsumers want from employment. The 2015 survey revealed areas of importance to job candidates based on successful employee value propositions (EVPs) used by HR departments. Respondents perceived four areas of the greatest concern to those looking to find work with one company versus another:

---

[1] HCI Research and Allegis Global Solutions, "Innovative Talent Acquisition Strategies to Attract the Talentsumer," (white paper, 2015), findings of a survey conducted between March and April, 2015, 2, https://www.allegisglobalsolutions. com/en-gb/insights/white-papers/recruitment-process-outsourcing/north-america/ innovative-talent-acquisition-strategies-to-attract-the-talentsumer.

- Offering more developmental opportunities
- Providing ongoing feedback and coaching from managers
- Encouraging collaboration among employees
- Recognizing and rewarding high performance

We'll unpack each of these in a moment. But first, let's consider more deeply *why* these things may have grown in importance for up-and-coming generations. Consider the world they will inhabit. Barring a cataclysm, the human population will continue to grow, and competition for resources and the work that provides them will as well. Throw the effects of climate change into the mix, and they'll see even more competition for organic resources. The rural-to-urban trend will probably leave fewer jobs in outlying areas and create more in cities, where dense populations will vie for them, yet employers still may not be able to fully staff up from local pools. Travel or remote work will increase. And since the employment scene will be volatile, job stability will degrade even further from the thirty-years-and-a-gold-watch standard than it already has.

That's not enough? At the same time, according to the Human Mortality Database, people will be living longer lives. Half of all babies born from this point onward in developed nations are expected to live past one hundred years.[2] Yet, we continue to pursue our working lives as our parents and grandparents have done—enjoying a single major career path to a certain age, say sixty-two or sixty-five, and then retiring on money previously saved and invested. How many people in current and future generations will be able to afford

---

[2] The 100-Year Life, "Oldest Age at Which 50% of Babies Born in 2007 Are Predicted to Still Be Alive," accessed February 21, 2019, http://www.100yearlife.com/the-challenge/.

retirement barely halfway through their lives? How many will be forced to change jobs or careers many times and start over building skills, income, and future plans?

In answer, today's Talentsumers want to be able to appeal to a variety of employers in more than one niche. So, they seek to associate with companies that provide continuing education, training, and support for the work they are doing— real opportunities to push themselves and develop new skills and interests. Given the future of sixty-plus years in the workplace these younger generations face, I don't blame them!

Engaging Millennial Stars—What the Stats Tell Us: Andy Partridge, COO, Link Humans

"71% of the Millennial workforce say[s] they're either not engaged, or actively disengaged, in the workforce today."
—2016 Gallup Report: How Millennials
Want to Work and Live

Compared to other generations, there are actually fewer Millennials who are actively disengaged (16 percent). So, that leaves 55 percent in that middle group— "not engaged"—and they're turning up every day at work saying, "Show me why I should be." What do they want? Not surprisingly, "meaning and purpose" topped the list. My experience working with young people is that they want to work for purpose-driven organizations, but also to feel a connection to individual purpose and a sense of journey. They want to feel that they can develop and move forward.

I've had the greatest pleasure working with Millennials and helping them to envision success. I'm always told that they feel life moves so fast and they deal with so much information that they rarely have the opportunity to take a step back and explore what really matters to them. So, I take the time to connect them with what their success could look like.

Gallup also reports that the top priority for 87 percent of Millennials when looking for a job is the opportunity to learn and grow. Of those who've had such opportunities, 68 percent plan to stay with their current company another year. Yet, less than half acknowledge that they *have* learnt something new or had the chance to do so in the past year. And just one-third who did felt the effort was worth their time—in other words, it fell short.

They may feel their only option is to quit: *93 percent said the last time they changed roles they had to leave their employer.* So, it's critical for us to help Millennial employees understand that they don't need to go somewhere else to keep developing in a relevant manner.

Millennials Are Not Job Hoppers ...

... if they're engaged in the right ways. But employers risk losing them if they don't actively address the engagement issue.

According to Gallup, 72 percent of Millennials who said their managers help them set performance goals are engaged. We can infer, then, that they want to be clear about expectations, and they want to work collaboratively so they can own those expectations. They're saying, "Don't make me guess," and "Inspire me with what *great* looks like. Tell me who are the great performers." In a fast-paced world, they don't have time for trial and error.

Millennials want to understand what they do well and what comes naturally to them, and to work out how best to achieve their goals using their strengths. They want to understand themselves so they can do great work. If we can't help them do that, they'll look elsewhere. According to the report, *"6 in 10 are open to other job opportunities and plan to be with another employer 1 year from now."*

So, how can we engage them? Meet these needs that Gallup has documented:

1. Millennials don't just work for a paycheck; they want a purpose.

Work must have meaning. These workers prefer organizations with a clear mission and purpose.

2. Millennials aren't pursuing job satisfaction, they're pursuing development.

They can take or leave the bells and whistles. They really crave development that will serve them in the long term.

3. Millennials don't want bosses—they want coaches.

Interactive oversight sets them up for success. Bosses need to help them understand and build on their strengths.

4. Millennials don't want annual reviews—they want conversations.

They've grown up with continuous feedback in real time, so daily connects are ideal. These don't have to be face-to-face meetings; quick texts and emails are fine.

5. Millennials would rather develop their strengths than fix their weaknesses.

Organizations need to maximize the strengths of their Millennial workers in order to keep their stars. Only about one-quarter claim that managers focus on their strengths, but when this does happen, about three-quarters say they're engaged.

6. Millennials see work as a part of—not separate from—their lives.

They ask, "Does this organization value my strengths and help me do great work every day?" Since employment consumes the major part of their lives, the answer had better be *yes*.

It's clearly time to address the engagement issue, as it could become a very expensive problem. Gallup says that Millennials are expected to make up 75 percent of the workforce by 2025.

Our job candidates and employees want the right to guide their working lives into new territory. They're serious about it. If they're with you now, they want the tools to perform a cost-benefit analysis of how their investment in you is paying off. If they're considering joining your team, they'll want information at their disposal to help them gauge the potential relationship, on their terms. Think about how you can answer the big questions that will help them plot the return on their investment, such as:

- How much and how fast can I learn?
- How challenging, rewarding, and exciting does the work remain?
- How much of my time is spent doing great and important work?
- How much personal success do I achieve—however I choose to define success?
- How easy is it for me to achieve what you ask?
- How easy is it to achieve what I want?
- How well, or poorly, do you use the assets I provide?

These are not necessarily "new" human desires. They are simply louder iterations of fundamental needs that are intrinsic to our nature. We hear plenty of business leaders lauding the work of Daniel Pink, a business writer and thinker who determined that **autonomy, mastery, and purpose** are all elements of fulfillment that motivate and engage workers.[3] And we want to think that our organizations provide opportunities in those areas. But how accessible are they? How easy is it for our employees to structure their work days (autonomy), excel in their roles (mastery), and contribute to something larger than just quotas and deadlines (purpose)? In the

---

[3] Daniel H. Pink, *Drive: The Surprising Truth About What Motivate Us* (New York: Riverhead Books, 2009).

midst of those pursuits, how easy do we make it for them to do their jobs really well and do their very best work?

These are not just abstract questions. For instance, a key gripe by workers— who are likely among the roughly 66 percent of the workforce who are not engaged or are actively disengaged, as recently reported by Gallup[4]—is that policies and processes hinder the completion of their tasks. Little roadblocks add up to big dips in morale. As an example, how about companies that still require expense reporting by stapling receipts to a piece of paper that they hand in at the end of the month? You no longer need to rope your kids into a monthly "arts and crafts project" to do that for you. There's an app for that! We can make life easier for those who travel or entertain by using one.

The other shift in younger-generation employees is a natural extension of the work/life balance debate. Now that the majority of people are always connected and, therefore, always with work on their minds, they rightly feel the separation of work and life is bogus. This is what lies beneath the movement toward creating more holistic and satisfying company cultures. Yes, great culture helps businesses financially, and this trickles up or down to employees. But workers now understand that they contribute their personal as well as professional gifts to employment. The equation demands that they then receive a measure of their personal satisfaction from the arrangement.

Much of appealing to the Talentsumer mentality is connected with cultural improvement. So is the endeavor of optimizing our workforces and work processes. We should be looking to revolutionize

---

[4] Jim Harter, "Employee Engagement on the Rise in the U.S.," Gallup News, August 26, 2018, https://news.gallup.com/poll/241649/employee-engagement-rise.aspx.

all of this now, so that we don't fall behind the steady march of technology and changing demographics and values. A vast break with the past is here, whether we like it or not. Getting to a state of organizational readiness will help us cultivate the segmented talent and work landscape that lies just outside our windows.

CHAPTER 3

Talent Integration: Where Companies Are Leading and Falling Short

Perhaps the biggest change affecting workers right now is the corporate move away from hiring regular, full-time employees. That norm has splintered into several segments of contingent hiring, including long-term affiliations with contractors and piecework done by short-timers. In response, job candidates have made adjustments. Most companies have not—or have not done so fully enough.

One mistake is to treat outsourcing as an HR or Procurement fad. Another is to attribute it to workers' growing preference to fly under the radar in the gig economy. Both of those ideas are simplistic. Outsourcing grew in popularity during the last economic downturn as a way to save on hiring costs. When greater benefits in productivity became apparent, the practice only increased in value. This doesn't mean that employers prefer contingent hiring, but they see the need to adapt to it. And most workers do not want dead-end, short-term gigs, but exciting projects or careers that can span different segments of the work world. This is why we are seeing more movement between jobs, and why employers are beginning to rethink how to fill their own needs with a series of talented people instead of just one long-term employee.

I believe the swift growth of the contingent workforce is not merely a trend, but the next plateau. And the movement toward that resting place is being propelled by companies seeking leverage, along with workers seeking greater flexibility. As we begin to reimagine the way work works in our companies, we'll need a more centralized and scientific means of acquiring and managing talent of all stripes.

This won't just happen business by business, as redundant strategies will waste valuable time and resources. Instead, **managed service providers** (MSPs) and **recruitment process outsourcing companies** (RPOs) will step in to synthesize searches and marketing efforts. They'll attract, screen, monitor, and process talent from all sources, all in one place. Of course, individual companies will need to echo some of this in-house by adjusting marketing methodology and internal policies that govern different classes of employees. Let's take a closer look at what's going right and wrong in these areas now.

New Recruiting Strategies

The immediate task for employers is to appeal to job candidates on their level—but this is where many organizations are struggling. Those that still rely on the old ways designed during the employer's market are already missing the boat. And the crew

Hiring organizations need to position themselves not as companies that serve only their own interests, but as talent platforms that allow individuals to do their very best work.

is not just limited to rank-and-file staff. Competition is high for qualified leaders, particularly in science, technology, engineering, and mathematics fields. Candidates for these jobs share the same augmented expectations of employers. To survive, companies will need to construct new recruiting criteria that meet the needs of Talentsumers. They must answer candidates' questions in their outreach efforts: *Will this company help me grow professionally? Does this business align with my personal and ethical goals and values?*

In the eyes of workers, if these needs are met, a business will earn their labor, their expertise, and their loyalty. A paycheck alone no longer bestows permission to direct workers' lives and efforts. Hiring organizations need to position themselves not as companies that serve only their own interests, but as talent platforms that allow individuals to do their very best work. The payoff for platform creators will be the ability to compose high-performing teams that respond nimbly to changing workloads and goals, leading to organizational readiness and, ultimately, business growth.

So, how do we sell this idea to both sides? By aligning our internal brand with Talentsumers' personal brands. Organizations can't expect to just post their jobs and hope the right individuals apply; instead, they must actively reach out to the right audience and showcase how their company offers the experience that candidates want from their employer. Professionals involved in talent attraction and retention—both in HR and among their talent acquisition partners—need to become world-class marketers. The formula is the same as consumer marketing: if we get their attention, turn it into attraction, convert them into "customers," and cultivate loyalty with great customer service ... we'll make them ambassadors for *our* brand.

Employee Advocacy: Craig Fisher, Marketing/Employer Branding Leader, Allegis Global Solutions

I was hired to improve the employer brand of a Fortune 500 legacy software firm that was moving to becoming a cloud technology company. The old ways of the business included many acquisitions and subsequent layoffs, and the company suffered a poor reputation on places like Glassdoor and anecdotally among tech candidates and salespeople.

From an ADWEEK research project, we understood that 92 percent of consumers say they trust recommendations from an individual more than the same content delivered by a brand. So, we decided to give our people—our most interesting selling point as an employer—a voice, and the encouragement to use it. In this way, we could grow our prospective talent pool and allow our job candidates to get to know us better as people, not just as a brand. We implemented an employee advocacy platform specifically for recruiting purposes, and the results were phenomenal.

We started with eighty seats on the platform, which is a little less than 1 percent of our global headcount, but which allowed a wide range in advocates. Seats were divided among a mix of recruiters, HR leaders, executives, hiring managers, marketers, and externally influential tech leaders at the client.

Our content strategy consisted of posting one piece of content per region, per workday. Timing for push notifications to employees was considered for maximum impact for each region.

The content mix considered business objectives for the client's employer brand, using a "5 gives to 1 ask" ratio:

40% Interview/Resume/Career tips
20% Diversity in tech
25% Tech industry news/highlights
15% Job posting

Getting employees involved in spreading your company's authentic culture and helping to attract more great talent to the organization isn't as simple as flipping a switch to turn on some software. It involves training, a well-devised roll-out plan, and regular communication. If done properly, this work pays off.

The Results: We saw a vast increase in the network growth of our champions (the eighty brand advocates picked for initial proof of concept). This meant more eyes on our employer stories as well as our people, leading to increased referrals, a key goal.

Five months after launching the program, the quantitative results were as impressive as the qualitative feedback from users. We achieved over 1,000 percent more audience growth than the growth over the same time period on the client-owned careers social media channels. This boost in audience for our content resulted in a 33 percent increase in its total reach.

With this augmented reach, our employer brand content was undoubtedly more trusted when shared by our employees, as we saw in comparative engagement data. Articles shared through the new platform to users' social channels had 68 percent more clicks on average than those shared by our careers accounts on social media and resulted in a 70 percent boost in total clicks.

To tie these incredible results into a return-on-investment, we compared paid media market rates to the value of added content marketing through employees' networks, via the program. We learned that it nearly matched the market value for CPC (cost-per-click) and CPM (cost-per-impression). When comparing the market value to the new platform costs, we saw a 344 percent ROI in CPC and a 2,329 percent ROI in CPM! We estimate that we saved in the region of $300,000 over five months, when compared to traditional advertising costs.

And how do we do this? It starts with putting together a killer employee value proposition. At its core, the EVP is a virtual crossroads. It is the place where the company's story—its history, mission, vision, and values—meets the candidates' needs. And this is the first area in which many organizations are falling short. As that 2015 survey (HCI Research/Allegis Global Solutions) of HR professionals shows, internal roadblocks are largely to blame. Those surveyed found the most difficulty in developing and presenting their EVP and employer brands due to:

- Insufficient staff to perform marketing work
- Low administrative priority on the issue

- Overall resistance to change

Resistance to change? Gee, that sounds familiar. And it demonstrates how damaging this emotional response to a market reality can be. Adversity to change is a drag on agility. It prevents businesses from making the quick moves they will need to make to stay viable. As acquiring the best talent becomes more challenging, companies that fail to take a proactive approach to change and other internal hurdles will also fail to attract the key workers they need to rise above the competition and achieve their business goals.

Is your company ready to appeal to Talentsumers across all sourcing channels? Few businesses have integrated frameworks in place for reaching them. Traditionally, human resources departments have been charged with managing full-time staff, while procurement departments or distinct business units handle contract talent. This division will become increasingly harmful to staffing efforts, and a merger or task-sharing initiative is necessary to reach all potential and available job candidates.

Adjusting policies to better navigate sourcing channels entails a clear-eyed analysis of internal and external hiring-related data. But in a 2018 study by Allegis Group, nearly one-third of HR managers claimed a lack of visibility into the total demand for talent across the organization, as well as into the total available talent supply.[5] Astonishingly, more than one-third of respondents also said their

---

[5] Allegis Group, "The New Meaning of Talent," (white paper, 2018) presenting survey results from 1,000 human resources professionals, conducted in association with Research Now SSI in 2018, 15, https://www.allegisgroup.com/en/insights/workplace-trends.

companies have no analytics system in place to measure their success in talent acquisition.

This is a grave concern to work quality and company finances. An inability to compile workforce data has consequences—such as extended hiring cycles and the cost of salaries set above market rate, as well as a drop in performance, work quality, and goal achievement. How can business and HR leaders make decisions to change course without the facts? Analysis of current data is a prerequisite for building a solid talent platform and the marketing strategy to promote it.

Employers will need far more than clever branding to achieve this state of readiness. They'll need to understand where their workforce is and where it needs to be, and to give these issues as high a priority as a balance sheet or a P&L statement. Companies benefit from an integrated talent approach with greater visibility, compliance, and cost management. But I believe the biggest gain is realized in the ability to own workforce design and take it to the next level. We'll talk about that in Part Two of this book. For now, let's look at additional mistakes to avoid in making your company's case to today's career and project seekers.

Competing for Talentsumers

Like shopping, these days work is something that can be carried out at our convenience, untethered from bricks-and-mortar headquarters. Whether our workplaces are fixed or remote, technology has removed the imperative to "go there." Trips to the copy machine and board room are becoming obsolete as nearly any action can be carried out at our desks or in our living rooms. It's no wonder, then, that employees consider themselves consumers of work, as the term

Talentsumer implies. Their behaviors in job searches and tendencies in the associations they make are increasingly mirroring what we usually see in the B2C sector.

Smart businesses are already using consumer data to drive the search for talent. This means tracking what is meaningful to them and what they consider perks versus make-or-break features of the companies for which they choose to work. Businesses that lack the attractive value of a strong employer brand and a reputation-building candidate experience are finding themselves at a hiring disadvantage. If organizations themselves do not develop brands through internal marketing platforms, users of rating websites such as Glassdoor and even Yelp will project them by default. In fact, if you are wondering where your enterprise stands, perform a generic search for employee or candidate reviews of your organization—it is fair to say that, for most companies, if that doesn't give you a sense of urgency, nothing will!

Empowerment = Increased Customer Service; TekWissen Group, 'The Senta Brothers'

As we all know employee empowerment gives performance-driven enterprises their competitive edge and we have experienced several instances related to it at TekWissen Group. Nurturing continuous collaborative learning and characterize performance-driven environment has helped us to rise & shine in this low barrier to entry business. It gives our employees the freedom, flexibility, and power to make decisions and solve problems which leaves our employees feeling energized, capable, and determined to make the organization successful.

We also made certain changes in 2018 after going through Accenture DSDP mentoring program to make our employees empowered. We had to do some major restructuring at TekWissen to reduce levels of the hierarchy in the reporting chain (increase efficient decision making and encourage accountability in the process) and be more customer & process focused.

Employee empowerment has given our employees a higher degree of autonomy and control in their day-to-day activities which has resulted in increased performance and engagement. It certainly resulted in process improvement, creating and managing new systems and tactics, and running departments with less oversight from higher-level management. We leaned on additional training with the goal to give necessary skills to carry out the additional task & necessary information on which they can learn to take decision independently. As a result, we saw more engagement and increased degree of accountability.

Simply Irresistible Organization model				
Meaningful Work	Supportive Management	Positive Work Environment	Growth opportunity	Trust in leadership
Autonomy	Clear and transparent goals	Flexible work environment	Training and support on the job	Mission and purpose
Select to fit	Coaching	Humanistic workplace	Facilitated talent mobility	Continuous investment in people
Small, empowered teams	Investment in development of managers	Culture of recognition	Self-directed, dynamic learning	Transparency and honesty
Time for stack	Agile performance management	Fair, inclusive, diverse work environment	High-impact learning culture	Inspiration
Cross-organization collaboration and communication				

> Traditionally too many steps in the hierarchy was over controlling process, systems and in few cases even their outcomes. Now, because of the changes, members of the team are more customer driven and are actively participating in problem solving and knowledge sharing.
>
> However, this does not mean that management relinquishes all authority, delegates all decision-making and allows operations to run without accountability. It requires a significant investment of time and training, especially from management, to develop mutual trust, assess and add to individuals' capabilities and develop clear agreements about roles, responsibilities, risk taking and boundaries.

Falling behind the talent curve causes real pain in the areas of profit and growth. According to Gallup's most recent survey on worker engagement, "organizations that are the best in engaging their employees achieve earnings-per-share growth that is **more than four times** that of their competitors"[6]—as well as 21 percent greater profitability. As money isn't everything, these businesses also enjoyed:

- Higher productivity
- Better retention
- Fewer accidents
- Healthier workers
- Better customer satisfaction

---

[6] Gallup, Inc. "U.S. Employee Engagement Trend," survey of 30,628 working adults across 50 U.S. states, conducted January–June 2018, https://news.gallup.com/poll/241649/employee-engagement-rise.aspx.

What is driving the growing competition for talent? Gallup points to factors in the job market that have enabled an increase in demands from workers: a rebounding economy improved consumer confidence and reduced unemployment and underemployment. As employees gained more choices, those who were disengaged could change jobs and leave unsatisfactory working conditions behind. They could accept positions with businesses offering more vacation time, better retirement plans, and flexible office hours.

It is up to employers to demonstrate that their work environments meet the needs and desires of sought-after talent. And a veneer won't do. This is why you hear so much about company culture presently. If a workplace and its foundations are not authentic reflections of great ethics and business practices, people sense that insincerity. Even if candidates are lured in by a positive message, promises that aren't kept won't serve to motivate and retain serious workers. And, given that tenures are becoming shorter, this devalues the investment that companies make in the people they hire.

Indeed, an effective integrated structure works both ways: as the percentage of contingent workers grows and tenure of employees decreases, companies must ensure they are agile enough to get the most out of workers in the time they are associated with them.

Does this mean that the HR emphasis on worker retention needs to be reevaluated? Not really. It need only be adjusted to take into account the new time frame under which employers are operating. For contingent workers who may only be with an organization for a short while, the old model of getting ROI over a lengthy period just doesn't work anymore—either for those who hire or those who work for them. Even when appealing to so-called permanent employees, who also aren't staying as long as they used to, both sides need ways to get that ROI far more quickly than in the past.

Good culture is one vehicle for that. You'll find myriad books and other resources about how to create, maintain, and improve the type of culture that employees crave. Instituting these things costs little but does require dedicated time and perseverance. Trying to cobble together the "look" of culture via flashy perks like living-room seating and free lunches isn't enough. A nurturing culture must be the genuine product and extension of a company's values and vision.

Please don't fall into the trap of sending the suits away for a long weekend retreat and coming back with inspirational quotes to post on the office walls! If your operation doesn't have the time to be systematic about culture, consultants with proven track records can help. Instead of relying on workplace trappings, they focus on a company's story and build on its strengths. They locate what is unique to a business and instill a search for like-minded individuals in the hiring process. This builds culture through people and past history; it creates a sense of permanence in an impermanent world. That effect surely resonates with Talentsumers.

Another important hallmark of an attractive ROI is thoughtful workflow and workforce design. As I mentioned earlier, making it easy for your team to achieve the goals you set for them takes a little thought and ingenuity. A salesperson who has the option of verifying business expenses by stapling little bits of paper to a large bit of paper or pressing a few buttons in a digital app will prefer the easier route. An executive who has to carry two cell phones because the company's model has a cumbersome interface will lose some measure of efficiency—and patience.

The hassle factor can be big or small. It pays to evaluate how your workflows and teams are structured and to remove obstacles. And getting feedback from employees may be the most valuable intelligence of all. Let them answer: *What can we do to make your work experience easier? More enjoyable? More meaningful?* Or, as Bill Jensen, speaker and author of *Simplicity*, puts it most powerfully: "How easy do we make it for you to do great work?" These are the questions we need to be asking, and our response to their answers must come in the form of action. We streamline protocols. Increase avenues of acknowledgement. Let our team members know that our purpose is as important to our operation as market share or profits.

Personal Employee Engagement

While planning a workshop at an organization I'll call Acme Company, I asked one of the supervisors in the customer service department to help me out. I said, "I really need access to your superstars. I'm running some organizational design workshops, and I'm looking to understand how work works here."

She replied, "I'd make sure you get Mary Smith in that group. She's phenomenal!" I asked what made her say that. She confided, "Mary loves this place so much that she's the first one here every morning. She gets in an hour before everybody else. She's so passionate. She'll be a great ambassador for the unit."

So, I invited Mary, and the workshop proceeded as I'd expected, until we got to this exchange:

> Bruce: How easy does Acme Company make it for you to do great work?
>
> Mary: "Oh, Jeez, this place sucks!
>
> Bruce: *(gasps, regains control)* Interesting. You mean, they *don't* make it easy?
>
> Mary: Hardly. I've got two children, four and two years old. I have to get them to kindergarten every morning by six-thirty, even though school doesn't start until eight. They open an hour early for me, and I drop off two kids with sad faces.
>
> Bruce: But, what does that have to do with work? Why do you have to drop the kids off so early?
>
> Mary: Because Acme's IT systems are so archaic that when everybody else logs on, it takes me ten times as long to do anything. So, I get to the office an hour early to get lots of work done before anybody else logs on to the network."
>
> *R-ight.* Actually, Mary *was* a superstar. Besides her other duties, Mary was speaking to Acme's customers every day and representing the company's brand—despite how inefficient its work process was. The company was making it so hard for her to get work done that she was giving up an hour of life with her kids every day, thanks to a horrible legacy system, not because she loved the company! That kind of quality amid that level of sacrifice will only last so long.

And we must mean it. Today's Talentsumers are some of the most discerning consumers out there. They have power, and they have choices. So, to leverage our employer brand, we must optimize how we get work done and by whom. Workforce planning, or more precisely, workforce design, must arrive at the most efficient and effective track. It becomes a part of great culture, both accommodating and driving it. These things are no longer "nice to have." They are essential.

To appeal to Talentsumers and move a business forward, I believe companies must adopt a holistic approach to how work is performed. They must identify which core skills and roles they need within their organizations to make them who they are. In what positions can you hire "permanent" workers? Which positions, by the very nature of the skill set required, will best be filled by contractors, consultants, or even machines? When we ask, answer, and act upon these questions, we help to solidify our company cultures. It is that solid standing, coupled with a desire to continuously innovate, that Talentsumers are looking for.

Part Two

WHAT DOES READINESS LOOK LIKE?

The New Employer

CHAPTER 4

Matching Workers to Work

While today's knowledge workers have negotiating strength, the choice of how to get the work done and by which type of worker is yours. Consensus is growing that this decision, which you'll make again and again, is the key to leveraging your business in the evolving competitive landscape. This choice is inseparable from the outcome you wish to achieve. Base your hiring decisions on your achievement goals, rather than vice versa, and you'll come out ahead. We'll look next at how forward-thinking organizations are doing this. It's goodbye to the old model of hitching your business wagon to a handful of serious employees and letting them set the pace and destination. Instead, it's your destination, your north star —that virtual place to which you want your work to carry you—that will drive your people selection.

So, we've got two dynamics on which to drill down—assessing our work needs and assessing our talent options. These two major tasks will help you break through to a new way of readying your company for the challenges to come. Such comprehensive evaluative actions, however, are the kinds of things that executives and HR staffs claim not to have the time to pursue. Well, it's time to make time! A great impetus may be to create a budget with real dollars invested for a group of internal superstars to focus dedicated time on this imperative—or hire a consultant or talent solutions firm to guide those efforts. Do not tap a bunch of your folks to do this while they continue in their day jobs—it will take too long, or if it doesn't, the quality and depth of thought may not be there. You haven't got the luxury of leisure here. Once you spend real money on it, the time and focus may magically arise!

In the second part of this chapter, we'll investigate how organizations are seeing their workflows anew by breaking them down into their salient parts. This tells them which type of worker will best do the job. First, though, let's return to the focus of every company that is not a sole proprietorship: job candidates that will become employees in some capacity.

> *The real job now in the world of Human Resources is to fully understand how work works inside your company.*

We've peeked at the basic "bodies" of talent—permanent, contingent, and automated. Now, let's dive into each of those categories to enumerate your hiring options by source.

Sourcing Options

INDIVIDUAL WORKERS	GROUPED RESOURCES	AUXILLARY
EMPLOYEES	SERVICE PROVIDERS (SOW)	INTERNS
TEMPORARIES	OUTSOURCED	VOLUNTEERS
CONTRACTORS (ROLE BASED)	CRAFT COLLECTIVES	DIGITAL WORKERS
CONSULTANTS (TASK BASED)	CROWDSOURCING	ROBOTS

You can see by the graphic above how many more talent verticals are available to tap than there once were. More choices afford more flexibility on the hiring end. But they also demand more informed decision-making than was necessary in the old days. That will take a deep understanding of each source and what each type of worker needs and wants, plus a continual awareness of the nature of the work to be done. These are areas in which HR and Procurement must scale up their knowledge immediately, if not sooner. Let's move through the alternatives step by step, to get you started. The key here is to make informed, empirically based decisions as to which channel(s) to tap into for which type of work. That means collecting and analyzing the data regarding how discreet pieces of work have fared best in the past. Track how projects are resourced and why particular resource mixes are better than others. At Allegis Global Solutions we are developing **DocuSift**, an AI-enabled analytics application to rapidly extract unstructured data from various Statement of Work document types and uses machine learning models to convert it into structured data to identify what is being bought, who is being used, and what is being paid. Further, this brings line of sight to potential risk related to contractual terms as well as worker classification.

The alternative is like playing Plinko, where the disk falls...

Individual Job Candidates

Yes, **permanent, full-time employees** may still form the backbone of our organizations. But how we connect and interact with them has evolved. As we rethink our departmental structures and hiring methods, we must resolve to let go of the old ways that we've clung to simply out of sentimentality or inertia. Move from a command-and-control to trust-and-verify approach. Particularly in compact or family-run businesses, the paradigms that worked yesterday are often preserved as we focus on other, more swiftly changing issues, such as technology-related decisions. Should we not start any assessment of human resources with our fundamental attitude?

Perhaps we are prioritizing the "permanence" of the relationship over the quality of that association. Recall that self-reported worker engagement hovers at 34 percent. Combine that with the trend in shorter tenures of full-time employees. According to *Lead the Work: Navigating a World Beyond Employment*, an informal look at LinkedIn profiles shows that many people moving between full-time jobs do so after one, two, or three years.[7] Authors John Boudreau, Ravin Jesuthasan, and David Creelman point to this statistic to call for a greater emphasis on work*flow* design, in order to optimize the work*force*. They rightly hold that creating a better relationship between the work itself and our internal structures will automatically strengthen worker engagement. They do not see engagement itself as management's end goal, however, but as the means to improved work outcomes.

This is really a chicken-and-egg scenario; we cannot separate better organization of work processes from employee satisfaction and motivation. Indeed, that 2018 Gallup research links greater performance opportunities—the chance for workers to do what they do best, develop skills, and be included in decisions that affect them—to greater business outcomes, profits, and importantly, worker retention. So, as we consider how to choose

---

[7] John W. Boudreau, Ravin Jesuthasan, and David Creelman, *Lead the Work: Navigating a World Beyond Employment* (Hoboken, NJ: Wiley & Sons, Inc., 2015), 28.

and cultivate our full-time employees, I believe maximum engagement should be our goal. We put our largest investment into these people; we should get the most from our time with them. Arranging our workflows and HR policies toward that goal should be part of an ongoing effort to nurture company culture to appeal to these workers. There is much written about getting between 10 and 20 percent more out of engaged people through the increased discretionary effort they bring to work. My view is that 100 percent of effort can be discretionary. You want people waking up with a smile on their face and giving their all. Hire those people and focus on setting them up for success!

The same is true of part-time, outsourced, temporary, or seasonal workers. We cannot afford to marginalize part-time or informal staff. Just think, when was the last time your CEO handled a brand promise directly with a customer? Never! But customer service centers that represent you handle that important task all day,

> *"It doesn't make sense to hire smart people and then tell them what to do; we hire smart people so they can tell us what to do."*
> —Steve Jobs

every day! We should build some degree of autonomy, mastery, and purpose into every job description and work task. In other words, what's in it for them? In reaching out to either full- or partial-time talent as job candidates, it will be necessary to convey to them the company's story and employer value proposition in a compelling way, which we'll talk more about in Chapter 6.

"Give Me Feedback": Craig Fisher, Marketing/Employer Branding Leader, Allegis Global Solutions

I was tasked with helping to improve the candidate experience of a multinational, publicly held corporation headquartered in New York City. It was ranked among the largest independent software corporations in the world, reporting over four billion dollars in revenue for 2016. In a year, this company receives an average of one hundred thousand applications, of which only 12 percent were reviewed.

Because the majority of applications received were not relevant to the roles being applied for, the Talent Acquisition team considered their review as time wasted and siphoned away from finding qualified candidates to fill the positions. This meant that thousands of applicants annually were being ignored, creating a bad candidate experience and detracting from the brand we were striving to embody. And we were unable to fully realize the ROI on marketing investments.

To close the proverbial black hole and improve the company's candidate experience, we determined that every applicant needed to be reviewed and receive a timely response, either by email or phone. But how to go about that?

We resolved to build an in-house, offshore team of talent assessors in one of our recruitment delivery centers to perform application screens of all candidates who applied through the company's applicant tracking system. After initial screening, we let candidates who were not considered the right matches for specific roles know, but also invited them to join our talent community. That way, we could track their careers and remind them of other positions as they became available. Why waste that first contact? Those who did meet the requirements and disposition of the role continued along the recruitment workflow.

The results were exceptional:

- 100 percent response to job applicants within 2.5 days
- 25,000+ applications reviewed during the first quarter
- 60 hires made from the pool that might have gone previously unreviewed
- a more accurate candidate database and source of qualified applicants' data
- Annual cost of the program: less than $20,000

Contractors and consultants represent a growing sector of the in-house workforce, yet our hiring and management approach may not have changed since we first dipped into that talent pool. With the speed and volume of projects increasing, we may hire and end relationships with many more of these contingent workers in a year than we once did. Can we really look at them as though we are speed-dating over cups of coffee, perhaps never to meet again? We must revisit how ongoing or short-term relationships with people who work by the project mesh with our overall HR policies.

Instead of treating these free agents like ships passing in the night, we should welcome them into the fold as fully as we would our permanent staff, for reasons of engagement but also security. They may become privy to all sorts of sensitive or proprietary information, and correctly offboarding each contractor—such as ending IT access and conducting exit interviews—is a must to safely provide closure to the relationship. The exit interview will reveal how well you fulfilled your end of the bargain, but it also affords one last chance to leave a positive impression of the company with the contract worker. You may need their services again someday. They may be able to provide referrals to key talent for other roles.

Don't Get Mired in Talent Denial: Barry Asin, President, Staffing Industry Analysts

The talent gap has turned into a talent crisis. That means that the old days of "post and pray" to get the traditional, permanent employees that you need for a role are slipping into the past. Ignoring important and growing pools of talent will only sell your company short.

We talk to many leaders struggling to ensure they have the right talent in the right place at the right time. The forward-thinking companies we see are taking a more strategic, total talent approach to getting the right type of worker for the work that needs to be done. To do that requires breaking down some of the old silos that separate Human Resources and talent acquisition for traditional employees from Procurement and contingent workforce management for temporary workers and contractors.

Sometimes the answer may be a traditional employee, but many times the best answer is a consultant, a freelancer, a temporary worker, an outsourced service, or perhaps a talent cloud of remote workers based anywhere in the world. All those options are more easily accessible and manageable than ever before. The critical talent project in the years ahead is to arrive at an integrated process for sorting through talent options to determine how to get the best quality, at the lowest total cost, in the most efficient manner.

In short, developing permanent relationships with temporary hires is good business practice. After a satisfying experience, they may well become cheerleaders for your employer brand. You certainly don't want them bad-mouthing the company on social media or sharing company secrets out of spite. So, as you look at contract candidates, consider them as potential members of the company, for however long they might be there. This means onboarding them in the same way as permanent staff as well, including aligning them with the company mission, vision, and values, providing a peer mentor, or other ways of integrating new hires into the staff as a whole.

In other words, the candidate experience should be similarly welcoming, no matter the hiring status. And, again, your work*flow* design will drive your work*force* decision on when to bring in those contractors and consultants—workers whose skill sets are not available in your permanent staff makeup. You'll reach out to them with something similar to your EVP, but not exactly the same; contract workers tend to be more interested in the project first, and which company name is above the door second. You need to be thinking of an assignment value proposition (AVP), noting how rich even a short association with your company can be for them in building their value for the next assignment. But *who* will be charged with oversight? As I suggested earlier, a collaboration between HR and Procurement will best facilitate this more integrated approach. It may come down to who in your organization truly understands the type of contractors you are using, and this requires a deep understanding of what the *work* needs. As Boudreau et al. relate, "A leader who is skilled in managing the relationships brings an immense amount of power to an organization,"[8] and that is because they know precisely *how* to match the worker to the work.

Group Candidate Sources and Unsalaried Workers

Suppose you don't want to keep throwing out one fishing line to reel in contingent help, either for recurring projects, recurring periods of high demand, or hard-to-find skills. Maybe you find a new business opportunity that you haven't yet tested, with a workflow that isn't yet defined. Selecting from a bigger or smaller talent pool than the general public may help you out.

Traditional staffing services and craft collectives concentrate candidates from specific talent verticals. You can spell out the skill set and mentality you are looking for, and professional recruiters will perform the initial search for you using their networks. Or, you can tap a collective, such as a professional group of graphic artists or software coders within an online platform. Collectives offer a

---

[8] Boudreau et al., *Lead the Work*, 43.

measure of quality control, as their brands and reputations are built on their combined expertise and value.

Consider how your AVP can appeal specifically to these two types of groups. Your specific project and culture may outstrip competitors recruiting by "just" using their brand name. Your business reputation can add credibility or integrity to a collective's brand, in addition to what you can give to individual workers. We'll look more closely at how to build and highlight your AVP and EVP in Chapter 6, but you can gain insight into how well they attract candidates in the group sphere by surveying and holding exit interviews with both the individuals and those that represent the collective or staffing agency.

Another burgeoning talent source arises from the **company alliance.** Friendly relations with peer businesses or even firms in divergent sectors represent your "library card" to loaner talent. Some strategic partnerships are made to increase investment power or to fuel collaborative innovation, such as alliances between Microsoft and Intel or Canon and Hewlett-Packard. Other pairings tap one company's reputation and expertise to fill a void in another organization, such as the Pepsico/Starbucks relationship that allowed the soft drink maker to add coffee-based beverages to its menu of market offerings.

The success they enjoy, however, comes from an increase in overall brain power. Suppose a marketing opportunity crops up and your company is in need of some animation experts. If you're not in the film business and you don't want to shell out money to a high-end video producer, why not borrow an employee from a well-known film technology company to assist your team? A big name from Pixar or Industrial Light & Magic will lend street cred to an in-house project that otherwise would have had "amateur" stamped all over it.

When to secure a talent loan should hinge not just on the tasks you need done but the quality level you seek. If your company does not excel at video production, find one that does. If your team can do the work but individuals in another company could do it more efficiently or more effectively, look into a borrowing arrangement. In the best of both worlds, an exchange of talent might be possible. Whatever the association, be sure to "adopt" that employee as one of your own for the agreed time period. That worker will grow during the time spent with your outfit, and you'll move ahead by gaining a much-needed skill.

Sometimes we have projects that are one-offs or our teams are too busy to attend to. It may not pay to hire or borrow a worker for a formal arrangement, or our usual hiring sources may have dried up, or the individuals we desire aren't available at the time. **Public talent platforms** offer a ready pool of freelance workers identified by their general skills, in areas such as writing and web design. For example, the online freelance platform Upwork allows individuals or businesses to hire freelancers through its web-based interface. Not a traditional staffing agency, Upwork acts as a facilitator for contractual transactions, providing the software management needed for employers and freelancers to connect and some support services to provide security to the experience. While contractors are not vetted by the platform, they are held accountable through an escrow payment system and job feedback postings that let prospective employers see how others reviewed the work of the candidates in question. This creates a democratized marketplace, with the best rising to the top.

Drink our own Champagne; Stephane Kasriel, CEO, Upwork

When it comes to embracing freelance talent within our own organization, we like to drink our own champagne. I empower all of our teams to hire contingent workers so that they are able to get more done. As a result, Upwork today consists of over 400 full-time employees and over 1,000 freelancers working on specialized projects - ranging from sourcing and product engineering to creative design. Every functional team within the organization leverages freelancers.

Oftentimes, freelancers have expertise that helps our core team learn new approaches. We find that incorporating freelancers into our talent strategy not only extends our bandwidth but helps us think differently and get new concepts to market faster all while being much more efficient and cost-effective than traditional approaches.

Similar platforms available to the public offer talent in single or related sectors, like IT and video production. Some of these, such as Topcoder and Tongal, double as **crowdsourcing platforms** that put the word out to all available talent, holding contests to determine the best candidate for a project. Others, such as Fiverr and MTurk, source workers for micro jobs or low-skill tasks from all over the globe.

If it's information gathering you need, a house-managed crowdsourcing project may be the answer. Tapping a large consumer network, for example, can provide requested data to drive decision-making or fill another need to circumvent hiring someone to do that work. Consider how Amazon's online shopping platform lets prospective buyers ask questions about products and purchasers answer them. This ingenious solution relieves the retailer of its obligation to provide that customer service!

At the other end of the spectrum lie organizations like Business Talent Group (BTG) that are resources for **high-end, on-demand talent,** such as independent management consultants, transformation experts, and project leaders. Similar to what we used to call interim executives, this relatively new business model is disrupting the well-established consulting firms in a big way as more and more companies start to take advantage of it. And, why not? They can access an army of "career consultants" who are choosing the independent route over the traditional consulting firm strategy of longevity to reach the heady heights of partner, only ever attainable by a few.

Yes, there's also something to be said for motivating people to work for free. Into this category fall **unpaid interns and volunteers.** It's easy to attract students or recent graduates to fill entry-level roles that will pad their résumés or look good on their college or grad school applications. Businesses in visible public sectors can take advantage of strong brand or issue loyalty by assembling volunteer workers. Local branches of the Humane Society, for example, are almost fully staffed by volunteers, while groups seeking political polling or petitioning may trade on their area of advocacy to draw unpaid telephone workers or signature gatherers. What business challenges do you have right now that a group of willing MBA students might want to weigh in on?

If you do ally with interns or volunteers, you'll need to take seriously the management of those groups, just as you would individual contractors or temporary workers. Get a system in place and track their performance and other metrics that you apply to more regular employees. Data analysis will be the overarching voice of reason for human resource recruiting and management in the years to come.

I include our auxiliary **robot and digital interface** friends among unpaid workers, although, of course, they will require economic investment to create and develop over time. Their efficacy will need to be tracked as well, so you might as well develop a management protocol for automated workers, while you're at it. While pursuing analytics will require more stringent performance oversight across all employee types, restructuring to provide visibility is a must. Our notion of whom or what to hire and when must be expanded from the old models, until we hit on a formula that works for our companies—at least for a period of time. Hiring practices are just going to be fluid for the foreseeable future, and we'll have to reevaluate them frequently.

Readiness in Talent Sourcing

As HR and Procurement leave behind their old inhibitions regarding contingent sourcing, they will open up to new ways of determining which workers to hire in which capacities. In the next chapter, we'll look at how to use workflows and project needs to identify the best matches. And *contingent* doesn't have to mean *outsourced*. Some of the types of talent listed above can be found within an organization, even while the individual still maintains their chief job status. For instance, why not post your temporary project needs into an internal platform and encourage employees to take on discrete tasks to push themselves and learn new skills, or use a skill that their current role isn't giving them the opportunity to?

One business that has embraced talent sourcing with a vengeance is privately held The Heritage Group (THG), an umbrella for thirty companies with a combined workforce of seven thousand across four major industries, including specialty chemicals and environmental services.[9] These guys need a wide range of expertise, to put it mildly. Sourcing talent for them? Why, no pressure at all.

Actually, the company's recent initiative responding to the shifting talent landscape lifted the lid on what would have become a pressure cooker had recruiters relied on the status quo much longer. Three steps swiftly improved their hiring position: 1) they moved away from predominantly permanent employees to explore hiring associations of all kinds, from all sources; 2) they surveyed staff to determine and use culture to support their EVP; and 3) they found ways to encourage their people to welcome change.

Leaders at THG suspended the old ways of hiring to match a limited job description and began selecting skilled candidates they perceived to be flexible enough to meet new challenges. They were willing to accept some risk and attracted people with expertise they believed they'd need in the future. They opened up to sourcing workers outside of their industries to increase the collective skill set of their workforce. Then, they gave those people what they wanted from an employer: the ability to provide input into how the work is done, as well as developmental opportunities to help build their careers. The Heritage Group has vigorous programs for building leadership

[9] Allegis Group, "The New Meaning of Talent," 13–14.

skills and "cross-pollinating" ideas among their member companies. Promotions can now take place across the full corporate structure, giving workers exponentially more ways to grow professionally within the larger organization.

All of this is positive. The willingness to question what a successful employer model had been led to an innovative talent strategy and new benefits for all the stakeholders. In the larger context, attracting the best talent *for tomorrow* is a competitive edge that will make member companies real contenders in their industries.

In the immediate future—which is *now,* remember—HR professionals and others associated with talent sourcing are going to have to take thinking outside the box to a whole new level. What was once a very regimented, segmented business practice has run smack into the flattening trend in management hierarchies. Rules for the sake of rules and protocol based on the status quo are out. Individual empowerment is in. The good news is that flatter landscapes within HR will allow for the equitable treatment of employees across sources and hiring designations. And having a basic protocol for all levels of staff will promote transparency and other goals of great culture.

Keeping an open mind about talent sourcing is a primary component of organizational readiness that will help you optimize productivity in your company. The other part of that equation is how well you've designed your work process. So, now that you know your people options, let's talk about the work.

CHAPTER 5

Deconstructing the Work

We are through the first leg of our "readiness" equation, with new insights into what great talent wants from us so that we can provide it and attract the best. But, as I mentioned in the first chapter, rather than projecting our business goals through the prism of existing employees' abilities, we must make our hiring decisions based on the ideal way to achieve our work objectives. The first step here is in understanding precisely what needs to be done. Then we can deconstruct the larger project into its main and sub components, giving us a clear picture of who might best do it—a full-time regular, a contractor, an algorithm, etc.—and we can move on from there to how to manage and support those workers to excel.

Taking tasks to their most basic level gives us valuable information. What to do with it? Two things: use the data to optimize workflows and processes; and analyze the data in light of performance indicators to determine which type of worker best suits the work. This gives us a need-to-know basis that includes the relevant project departments and the hiring departments. This will be a new or deeper responsibility for HR and Procurement, and one that some may fight. But since the balance has shifted—dispersing human resource management across many verticals instead of one or two—the way to remain agile is to clearly see what must be done, in order to utilize talent to the fullest.

Indeed, recall that 30 percent of HR professionals surveyed in 2018 acknowledged that the total talent demand across all departments was not visible or being centrally tracked. It follows that the performance components needed to achieve goals by that talent also are not compiled in one place. Good heavens! If one-third of us don't know whom we need to hire nor what they should be doing, many companies are sliding backward, not moving forward.

Know Who Works for You

While interviewing customer service agents at a telecom company, I asked how empowered they felt to show initiative and bring their best selves to work every day. I got an example of what was holding them back when a mature lady said she felt the level of financial discretion they had could be raised above the £20 that was in place.

After listening to her logical and succinct reasoning, I asked what her background was. She said that her "real" job was as a court magistrate, and that she only worked two evening shifts at the company to get to meet new folks and mix with some younger people. So, here we had someone making critical decisions during the day about people's freedom, while in her "hobby" job she had to consult a boss on disputes over £20!

Yet, you and I now have greater clarity on who *might* do the work. So, let's turn this sad statistic around by learning what our work needs *are* across the organization. Then, putting two and two together is not so far-fetched.

Breaking It Down

We have no trouble building job descriptions and workflows to meet project objectives. Deconstructing them simply involves reverse engineering. Yet, it is painstaking. And it should be. Why would we not want to understand every nuance of the work our people do? This is not a difficult task, overall. The tough part is figuring out what our response will be to what we learn. Is a process redundant? Wasteful? Already optimal? Are we missing key steps? Are they logically arranged? Leaders of project teams will have to take charge of analyzing and distilling the tasks that their staffs perform—or new processes in the making—to their essence. Then they must ask: do we have the talent in place to achieve these things? And further: do we have the right type of talent, being effectively motivated and rewarded? Here, close collaboration with HR management and work design architects, will be necessary. Team leaders will need to take what they know about the work hierarchy to those with the means to match it to the right people. Like never before, hiring professionals will be charged with understanding intimately what must be accomplished and how best to do it.

So, breaking down and evaluating work objectives will not end with the interested departments. These will wind up passing the baton to the folks who have that wide-angle vision into the company's total available and potential talent supply. The structure of the workflow and workforce, however, is not just HR's responsibility. How work and talent are organized impacts many parts of an organization and should be one of the most important pieces of any company's strategy. The war for talent is escalating, and my company (and our competitors, of course) work with customers every day across stakeholders in Procurement, Legal, and Risk—along with HR— to address the challenges and opportunities that are becoming commonplace in getting work done and growing their businesses. When we do this, then the beautiful alchemy of aligning workers and work can take place.

This arrangement also changes the balance of a leader's role. Going forward, instead of "just" leading the employees within, managers of business lines, departments, functions, or teams will be *leading the action and outcomes*. They must stay focused on business objectives even as they guide and support the people (and machines) working toward them.

Let's look at our operational and organizational designs however they are easiest to grasp—either from macro to micro, or vice versa. *How does work work inside your organization?* Could your CEO explain that? Who truly understands that flow chart? Ask these questions of the most knowledgeable people, whether they are boots on the ground or C-suite executives getting the big picture from a lofty perch. The goal will be to deconstruct projects or objectives into tasks, and tasks into distinct, meaningful activities. Even if you have already done this in the past, you will need to periodically revisit this process.

And you may need to go much deeper on this than you have before. Doing so will reveal relationships and, perhaps, novel ways of arranging the basic stepping stones of work to arrive at your objectives more quickly—or without getting wet. In this manner, your operational and organizational designs will remain flexible and easy to adjust to changing needs and talent channels. You might find better success by breaking assignments into pieces and delegating what one permanent employee once did to one or more types of workers who, together, can do a more efficient or superior job.

The information that you come up with can be fed into spreadsheets in order to methodically detail what each assignment involves and requires. You'll list hard deliverables, process steps, preparation steps, and "invisible" tasks such as creative thinking and trial and error. You may be surprised that the trajectory of work is not always linear!

Readiness in Work Design

A company that uses this information system to fill a void in its talent pipeline is German conglomerate Siemens, as John Boudreau discusses in his cowritten book *Lead the Work*.[10] Among its engineering and manufacturing portfolio, Siemens makes hearing aids. In assessing its underserved markets, corporate leaders identified children who use these devices. How to reach them? They knew what they needed: a marketing system aimed at kids. They knew that they *didn't know* exactly what it would take to construct that—and that they *didn't have* people with the expertise to first deconstruct it and then achieve it. While the company is world-class in technology, it does not have a Ronald McDonald or a Mickey Mouse to sell that technology to kids and their parents. But they knew who did.

---

[10] Boudreau et al., *Lead the Work,* 12–13.

A working partnership with Disney allowed for an exchange program with the kid-friendly enterprise's employees. Siemens had paired with the entertainment giant in the past to produce thrill rides for Disney's theme parks. Now, Disney workers were tapped to determine how to make Siemens's hearing aids appealing to children and how to implement a marketing plan. Disney's people homed in on the barriers to be surmounted— the clinical aspect of the devices and the stigma of using hearing aids that youngsters associate with being "different." To smash those perceptions, Disney's pros repackaged Siemens hearing aids along with a plush Mickey Mouse toy and a comic book featuring cool kids with hearing aids. By switching the product image from a medical device to a fun personal accessory, Siemens got a better foothold in a coveted market sector.

Instead of branching out into an area in which the corporation did not have deep experience, Siemens visionaries hit their mark more efficiently and with top-quality assistance by letting the work requirements define their hiring needs. This, of course, requires an acceptance of one's core mission and talent architecture. Knowing what the company does well and what is outside its scope is a valuable part of building and maintaining a functional business. *This* is what readiness looks like in the space where work design and workforce design intersect. It provides solid ground from which to make informed decisions about both sides of the equation: the work and the workers.

We're now one step away from integrating and optimizing these things. There's just one thing standing in our way. It's the last bastion of the old style of thinking: the wall dividing HR and Procurement.

Creating What People Need Before They Even Know They Need It: Dawn Tiura, CEO and President, Sourcing Industry Group, SIG University, and *Outsource* Magazine

The way Sourcing Industry Group (SIG) approaches "work" today grew from our shared experience in reading the book, *Demand: Creating What People Love Before They Know They Want It*, by Adrian Slywotzsky and Karl Weber (Crown Business, 2011). As the largest global association for executives who represent the procurement, sourcing, and outsourcing functions, we exercise a few of the authors' teachings almost religiously.

Fixing "hassles" is one; it addresses how to remove the frustration that people feel when they encounter glitches that they don't even recognize as hassles, but that put a negative spin on their experience. Slywotsky and Weber suggest charting a "hassle map" to identify every juncture in a process that could possibly be a friction point and finding a way to streamline and eliminate it. We apply this to how our constituents deal with SIG—whether requesting information, registering for an event, or submitting an abstract. We analyze and seek to remove all hassles for our delegates to make their association with us as frictionless and enjoyable as we can. As a result, it's amazing how many improvements we've made.

The other sacrosanct advice in the book is to "de-average the customer" to take into account their individuality. As a global association, this was a very important bias to overcome. By internalizing that one size does not fit all, we have recognized that we need wide variances in hassle maps. So, we work to create processes that meet the needs of all of our delegates.

> When we project into the future and eliminate hassles before people even acknowledge they exist, we become more attractive and can consistently grow our membership. This will allow us to represent deeper and wider cross-sections of industries and promote thought leadership from an ever-increasing range of viewpoints.

Breaking Organizational Barriers

Have you ever watched the studio credits roll after an animated feature film? There's the director, the assistant director, the effects designer, storyboard supervisor, texture artists, shaders, and animators. Then there are people who do lighting and fixing, and someone called the render wrangler (what the heck is a render wrangler?) And don't forget the caterers! The credits go on forever, listing multiple people in myriad roles. Do you think all those people are permanent employees of the studio?

Production workers likely crisscross between all sorts of hiring arrangements. I believe our organizations will one day be more like the movie business, in which hundreds of people come together, make a piece of art, and move on to the next project. We may maintain a nucleus of permanent employees that is routinely augmented on an as-needed basis with contingent workers. This new overall structure will be a crucial driver of agility, allowing us to optimize the work that our employees do. Within that agile state lies a prime source of business leverage: the ability to get more out of that key person than a competitor would. How? By the way the organization is set up.

Deconstructing the work must logically include deconstructing how we manage our internal support, as well as how we manage our employees. Now, you may want to grab ahold of something, as I am about to disrupt your worldview. *I challenge you* to start this conversation with all of your peers, across all departments:

> *What are we truly trying to achieve as an organization? What is our core business objective? Describe what our business will look like in two years if we have totally hit the ball out of the park.... How are we getting work done? With which type of people? What kind of contracts do we offer them? Let's take the time to ponder this, and truly understand what each of the functions inside our company are working toward, individually, and as a whole.*

Yes, knock it down to the roots. Ask, why are we here? What are our dreams? What do we want to be when we grow up? Rarely do we ask the fundamental questions at all, but especially in regard to *why* we do what we do every day. I challenge you to make a conscious effort, schedule the time, and think. Debate. Get some clarity.

Use a data visualization tool to create a talent architecture depiction of how you are getting work done now. Imagine a wall-sized graphic that shows your workforce, color-coded by geography, type of worker, volume, tenure, cost, etc. From there, create what you believe that same picture needs to look like in two years to achieve your business objectives. Now you can have the "How do we get from A to B?" conversation!

As they say, stop working *in* the business and work *on* the business. Ask your CFO where the company should be in one or two years, then ask the CPO, the CEO, the CTO—not about a vague wish or something off the vision or mission statement, but what it will take to get where you want to be. Then, talk it over. Understand the motivations of your internal departments. *What do they want their function to be known for in the next one or two years?* What is their branding? Their messaging? What talent do they have on hand? What kind of talent are they going to need to get to that point?

Have that conversation at every functional level. Human resources teams can be guilty of being the cobbler's children—not really comprehending the above or their function. This will bring them up to speed. Then, gather the whole leadership team and imagine a new structure. I mean, really be open to it. You might have to start with examining your inhibitions. How can you clear your head space to think about things differently?

You guessed it, I am zeroing in on an entrenched division that stands in the way of building your ideal talent base, organizational design, and hiring platform: HR versus Procurement. The two departments are, by design, at odds. Human resources types see investment in labor paying off by managing people properly to get the best performance. Procurement gurus believe returns are tied to speed, efficiency, and cost management, which may be achieved through work design or through stringent job requirements. The reality is that a combination of these things, driven by the company's goals and outcomes of the actual work completed, produce the ROI.

This ideological split can lead to a natural breakdown in communication between the two sides, and they often vie for control. Reinforcing this division throws a wall between efforts that have to be more closely aligned. It reduces visibility into an organization's total talent assets and needs. It operates from the false presumption that job status should drive the work. Instead, the people on both sides of that wall ought to be asking: *Do we have the right talent architecture to achieve our objectives? How do we get to that point?*

Outputs, Not Inputs: Bill Boorman, Advisor to VCs and Stand-up Comedian

"Work" is changing—appropriately, from jobs to work—and that means work design needs to change too. It's part of the shift from the old-school industrial management of command and control, going from measuring inputs and hours in attendance to measuring people on their outputs. Locations are getting more flexible; some work can now get done literally anywhere in the world, and I think we'll see the management layers above interchangeable project managers all but disappear. Companies need to rethink hiring for this new world, understanding that everybody is temporary, regardless of their contract.

The work deconstruction phase is an opportunity to end that competitive dynamic. Truly, the two functions are stronger together; one might notice opportunities or areas begging for improvement that the other would miss. It is time to let go of HR's "talent agnostic" limitations and Procurement's reliance on statements of work and let the talent decide how to contract. Recall the example of The Heritage Group opening its horizons to new sources for highly skilled people. Their leaders boldly made an intentional move from a corporate-centric to a people-centric means of getting the most from the best employees. Instead of losing control and becoming unmoored, the company found firmer footing with its large workforce.

Likewise, instead of promoting and searching against job requirements, you might start looking for personal skill requirements. Instead of calling for a permanent, full-time employee, ask: how do you want to work with us? Let the worker make the choice! This sets the tone, right off, promising to engage, motivate, reward, and empower. It demonstrates a supportive culture, rather than having that pasted into a job description somewhere.

So, let's assume you'll accept my challenge, rethink your organization's internal workings, and tear down the walls that blind your people to finding the right talent architecture and the right talent. When you open up the hiring landscape, you've got to be ready to see what's there. Most companies already do this in some areas.

Imagine that you're responsible for managing the real estate of your organization. Your CEO asks to meet with you next week to review the property portfolio. You have information on whether properties are owned or leased, length of committed contracts, cost per square foot, utilization levels, taxes, maintenance needs, etc. So, armed with that information, you can meet and have a great in-depth, strategic conversation as to how you might want to improve the mix of the portfolio over the next number of years. Right?

Let's think about the same question for people and how we're getting work done. Can you press a button now and get that information? Many companies don't even know how many people are working for them on any one day, let alone who they are, their skills, their desires etc. Some administrators have to consult LinkedIn to find out what skills they have in their workforce!

Once you've cleared the air and you're ready to look around, you'll want to answer a number of fundamental questions, including: *Do we even know who is in our organization? Which talent is there to tap for which functions?* You'll want to have a complete "dossier" on them, as you would any property in the company's portfolio. Survey their skills, preferences, passions, and goals. Then, you can act on this information plus your task breakdown to determine which assignments would be done best by one worker or another.

"We" Are the "They"

This is one of my favorite phrases about accountability. I came up with it while running a workshop for a large group of Human Resources country heads of a very large, global enterprise. I noticed that when I asked each of them to describe their company, most people did so in the third person: *They need a new mind set. They need to be more innovative. They need to give us more resources.* It was as though the people were not part of the organization, and were, in fact, in opposition to it.

I sort of lost it and roared, "Who the heck are the "they?'" I looked them in the eye and said, "YOU ARE THE THEY!" This hit them where they lived. By the end of the week, I had them chanting, *"WE ARE THE THEY!"*

Groups are made up of individuals; they don't become separate entities with greater numbers. Every time you feel you are going to use the *they* word regarding your company, please look in the mirror and realize it's your job to make it the *we.*

Use this same formula in assigning projects to employees by hiring status. By and large, HR has not gotten the big picture on the growing range of contract types. Start tracking this stuff! Job descriptions and levels of achievement fit into charts; use this data to see which hiring types are most cost-effective and productive by the task. This is truly letting the work lead the business. And it's proven effective, particularly when HR and Procurement collaborate. An Allegis Group report on contract talent showed an 11 percent gain in effective hiring practices that succeeded in getting the key individuals, timing, location, and pay point right—to the satisfaction of both departments—when the two departments worked together.[11] Further, involving business leaders in the sourcing discussions additionally influenced greater quality and efficiency in the people hired.

In fact, that study found that "the most highly effective organizations had shared authority between HR and Procurement across a variety of contract talent management processes. Involving stakeholders in various aspects of contract talent beyond their functional comfort zones correlated with above average results." One HR manager surveyed about the value of collaboration said it "helps to bring all parties that have a stake in contract labor to the table, work from the same plan, identify and address needs, priorities and issues holistically as opposed to being within a silo."

It's okay to tear down the walls. Everyone will still have their niches to fill. The point is to bring the work and workers closer together. As all of these changes coalesce, we must build a bridge

[11] Allegis Group and HCI Research, "When Worlds Collide: Procurement and HR Managing Contract Talent," (white paper, SIG, 2013), 9, 23, https://sig.org/when-worlds-collide-procurement-and-hr-managing-contract-talent.

between our organization's objectives and the candidates we invite to choose us as their employer or client.

Human Resources can play a big role here by examining how easy we make it for employees to do great work. Do we make people log expenses with crumpled up bits of paper receipts, or let them use an app? Do we limp along with sluggish computer programs, or do we invest more in IT and/or allow employees to use their own devices? Are we truly open to rapid innovation, and do we get out of the way when we need to? Word gets out. If we don't make it easy, we have no competitive advantage, and candidates will walk away. Our longtime staff will find greener pastures. Our businesses, like failing sit-coms, will have "jumped the shark."

As we attempt to fashion an alluring employer brand to woo great talent, we should continually ask ourselves, *How can the way in which we do business create self-motivation? How do we make it in the employees'/workers' interest to do great work?* If we court those answers, we will be able to attract talent of all kinds—from permanent team members to contractors to volunteers. This is all part and parcel of forming a robust and dynamic culture. To be successful, your employer brand and value proposition must come *from that culture.* As this all becomes absorbed into the organization's DNA, we move closer to organizational readiness, enabled by talent.

CHAPTER 6

Companies as Talent Platforms

W e used to say content is king. Now, conversation is king. When the topic of what it's like to work in your company comes up, what are your employees talking about—at least, when you're not within earshot? What's your story?

The employee experience both derives value from and pays into the company culture bank. This can be either a dynamic perpetual-motion machine—or a double-edged sword. If your culture evolves from your business ethos and practices, it drives your reputation as a great employer. If you've approached culture as a two-dimensional fix, inscribed on a poster on your wall ... you've just hacked off both of your lower limbs and are left without anything on which to stand.

So, to complete your third leg of organizational readiness and put together an all-encompassing talent platform, start with culture. Build an environment where everyone is empowered, enabled, encouraged, and rewarded to do their very best work. Get it right internally, and then articulate it. Find marketing channels to tell the world. This is who your company is, collectively. This is what your company does, and where it's coming from. If a job candidate can't summarize that in a few sentences, you aren't doing *your* job.

We'll take another look at culture now, as a vehicle to get at effective branding—effective because it is true, not hype. As an employer, a well-rounded organization should appeal to different talent markets. So, branding has to be inclusive but may be guided by several distinct EVPs and AVPs. These efforts at building culture and an employer and assignment brand must be rigorous and broad-minded, with the goal of reaching into every talent vertical in a search for the ideal matches. If you do not have the internal resources to direct toward specialty marketing, recruitment, and cultural development, find partners with that expertise.

This may sound like a lot of prep work, but the new employer can't get away with just placing a classified ad and hoping the right person walks in the door. To gain the competitive upper hand, companies will have to construct **total talent platforms** from which to dive into the great unknown. This is just the type of situation for which the Boy Scouts motto was coined. We may not be able to predict the future, but we can be prepared.

Abhishek Das, Director, Global Talent Acquisition Center, Allegis Group

We transitioned a team leader to manage the delivery team for a major client based on her strengths of being process oriented, people focused and being a strong disciplinarian herself. After working with the team for a few weeks, she realized, the need of the hour is discipline and team work. She wanted to focus

---

on getting discipline and accountability within the team. She concentrated on the small but significant things like people coming in on time, attending morning meetings, delivering the basic expected business results every day like candidate outreach, striking a specific number of conversations etc. Of course, she did not win any of the popularity votes by holding people accountable, however efficiency started to manifest within operations and there was another silent change brewing slowly that would transform productivity from good to great.

In people's resistance to accept change, they probably did not realize that they were actually unifying as a team. At least there was one common factor for people to get unified to among so many variables of working with different client stakeholders across multiple different geographies. While she saw people coming together, albeit against her, she worked with them relentlessly and helped them understand how this change would bring in opportunities for people, candidates and customers. She motivated the recruiters to compete internally with their own self and not externally, everyone strived to become a better version of themselves compared to the past.

It was wonderful to see the same team which had worked in their own ways for quite a while, rapidly unify to achieve the goals together. There were multiple times when the business peaked, the individual team members collaborated with each other to help realize each other's targets. Even team leads, reporting into this manager held themselves accountable not only to achieve team numbers but also worked overtime to wipe out other teams 'deficits. The team worked with a visible sense of unity towards creating opportunities for everyone, including our customers. As a result of this effort, our business with this particular grew by 34% YOY against a target of 15% and contrary to traditional belief she retained the majority of people with a less that 20% attrition over the last year.

It just goes to show, people do not leave organization when they are held accountable and micro-managed, people come together and go above and beyond when they are rallied together with a common cause and the manger's popularity score is now off the charts!

What Are You Famous For?

Your company story, like a national identity, should apply to everyone in the organization, even though your workforce may be diverse. This means that, despite generational, departmental, and personal divides, there should be one basic narrative that everyone can own. It's why you're able to assemble many different types of people to get on board your ship and all pull together.

Sometimes your story fits into a snappy slogan:

A business of caring. (Cigna)
You can do it. We can help. (Home Depot)
Make. Believe. (Sony)
The power of dreams. (Honda)
Don't be evil. (Google)

Sometimes a tagline can be interpreted in different ways:

Just do it. (Nike)

What, no direction? Who'd want to work for that boss? Of course, some might say, Wow, I love it when I get empowered and are measured on outputs and not micro-managed!

Sometimes a slogan does reflect your story, though, and it sets you apart from the other guys:

Think. (IBM)
Think big. (IMAX)
Think different. (Apple)

These are marketing slogans, yes; but they make an impact because they reflect the company's internal culture and values, as well as what they have to offer the public. If a business walks the talk, it's easy to sum up what they're famous for in just a few words. When "selling" our businesses to talent, we have more leeway for description, but we are held more stringently, perhaps, to the promise it contains.

If we are directing that message to Talentsumers, the promise is to employ their "whole selves"—as opposed to the alter egos that were left at the office door at 5 P.M. back in our parents' or grandparents' working days. As Tanya Axenson, Global Head of Human Resources for Allegis Group, describes it, our culture *is* our promise: "With a stated set of values," she relates, "our companies have a framework for fostering specific actions and practices that build an inclusive culture. From teaming up for volunteer activities to making time for person-to-person meetings that help us build relationships with colleagues, our culture is one where we recognize and celebrate both our commonalities and our differences. Each person can be their authentic self in such a culture, and that's a powerful value for our employees, our company, and the clients and candidates we serve. That's why our tagline is 'Opportunity Starts Here.'"[12]

Workers—and the particularly vocal Talentsumers—want to be a part of something, not cogs in wheels. Sure, they love the trappings of trendy culture: the pet-friendly cubicles and on-site workout rooms. But they crave what lies beneath all that. It pays to remind ourselves of Daniel Pink's insights into basic human needs—autonomy, mastery, and purpose.

Pink clearly took the time to explore where these abilities fit into the human psyche. Autonomy speaks to our need for control, but also something deeper than that. "When we enter the world," Pink asks in his book *Drive*, "are we wired to be passive and inert? Or are we wired to be active and engaged?"[13] Just asking that question reveals the answer, which normally developed, curious and busy toddlers display. Just as they want to direct their activities, so do more experienced adults. A desire for mastery emerges from engagement with a task or skill—it doesn't matter what it is. The better we get at doing it, the more fulfilled we feel. Look at video games, and how we strive to reach the highest levels of mastery there. This type of self-satisfaction increases our confidence and self-esteem—two qualities that help us do great work.

The emphasis on purpose in employees' lives has come to the fore as companies publicize their ethics, whether they are based on environmental, humanitarian, or other laudable concerns. Younger generations have grown up amidst these ideas, and many have taken

---

[12] Allegis Group, "The New Meaning of Talent," 8.
[13] Pink, *Drive*, 87.

stands that become part of their personal identities. An employer who furthers those moral convictions allows workers to be, as Axenson put it, "their authentic selves." That's a huge motivation today, as we are seeing in response to HR surveys. It bears out Daniel Pink's observation that "the most deeply motivated people—not to mention those who are most productive and satisfied—hitch their desires to a cause larger than themselves."[14]

As employers, it's not hard to find ways to breathe life into these concepts to truly serve people's emotional needs as we work alongside them. Let these goals be the bedrock of your culture and let all else stem from them.

For example, if you are IMAX, or Apple, or IBM, you have already built autonomy into the thinking part of employees' days. Autonomy says: *you are free to think, dream, innovate.* To get this result, an employer must give up some measure of control for the greater good. A searing example of why this is necessary is illustrated in Charlie Chaplin's 1936 film, *Modern Times.* The workday of his character, the Little Tramp, is tightly controlled, with every moment planned for him. In attempting to do exactly as his heavy-handed employer demands, the Tramp is force-fed lunch by machine and must work faster and faster to tighten screws on an assembly line— with disastrous (and hilarious) results. This worker, allowed zero autonomy, eventually has a nervous breakdown and winds up in hospital. Chaplin, far ahead of his time, realized that self-direction is not only a fundamental need, but that its absence is bad for business!

We'll surely want to find ways to let employees guide their own work habits and careers. How, then, can we also feed Talentsumers' hunger for mastery and purpose? By providing career development

---

[14] Pink, *Drive,* 131.

opportunities and putting great ethics behind what we do. All of this must go into the story that we tell job candidates—in social media blogs, in job posts, in phone interviews, and beyond. Continuity is key. At every phase in the application process, the company story must be shouted from the rooftops. This narrative should stand on its own merit, with no need to add, *Believe me!* Let the candidate determine how genuine it is or is not.

Feeling Down?

If you're having a bad day and you want to give yourself a laugh, pull your initial job description out of the drawer. How far off is reality from the job you thought you'd signed up for? That's not necessarily a bad thing. In fact, hopefully, it's because you are involved in loads of exciting, new projects above and beyond the original job description. But revisiting it will make you rethink how job descriptions are used inside your organization and whether they even have a place in today's world!

But, wait! We're not finished yet. Once an offer is accepted, this branding experience needs to continue—through onboarding, and through the first few months in which we engage new hires with our mission and methods. Make no mistake: today's Talentsumers will be reviewing the situation to see if what we've sold them is actually what the work experience is like. If it's not, in a candidate-driven market, they'll quickly move on. And they'll leave one-star reviews in their wake for the world to see—on Glassdoor, Indeed, Vault,

CareerBliss, Kununu, JobAdvisor, RateMyEmployer, TheJobCrowd, etc. Yes, there are a lot of them!

If you need help in getting your culture ducks in a row, think about some of the outsourcing avenues toward the end of this chapter. If, instead, your company story *is* ready for prime time, integrate it with your employer brand and proceed to put the finishing touches on your talent platform.

Readiness in Branding

Turning the story of your employee experience—and the larger *why* of the company—into a brand is crucial to your success in bidding for talent. It boils down to articulating where you are coming from and what you have to give to employees. As you continually refine this message, you'll use it to distinguish your work experience from other companies'. This will then be verified by your staff, one by one, in the story that *they* tell—online, to their coworkers, and to other potential hires. It would be nice if those two versions were one and the same.

Your brand will revolve around your employer and assignment value propositions, which may be geared to distinct subsets of the talent pool. You may be speaking to IT experts, factory workers, or remote contractors, depending on the job needs at hand. These people may be: urban, rural, or suburban dwellers; knowledge workers, intellectuals, artisans, or low-skilled laborers; and from any slot in a range of generations participating in the workforce. First, determine what you have to offer each of these groups. Then, specialize. As you work on these EVPs and AVPs, keep the thought process wide open. Don't stop at what you know is already working.

To arrive at "complete," well-designed EVPs, ask your current employees what your organization can be doing differently to make their jobs easier and to fully utilize their skills. Then do the same exercise with your contractors to create the AVPs. Although we may feel Millennials tend to speak out more often or more forcefully than members of other generations, they are driven by the same emotional needs as everyone else. Workers in any demographic appreciate more flexible working conditions, skill-building opportunities, and a meaningful purpose to their labor. In the new talent landscape, employers must not only meet these expectations, but show how their work culture does so. That is the goal of your branding message.

So, what does readiness look like in this regard? We are seeing more companies use this specialized form of marketing through social media channels and revamped corporate websites that feature their employer brand. Not so long ago, worker benefits, company culture, and the values on which a business was built were veiled— they were seen as either obvious or irrelevant to the public. Now, they are integral. And *not* articulating them, not *promoting* them, is a lost opportunity at leverage with two very important groups: potential and existing workers. The first, we want to attract; the second, we want to retain as long as the job demands it, and we want to retain their good impression as talent ambassadors *to others* once their tenure is up.

A strong employer brand has proven benefits. In research based on a study by LinkedIn, 85 percent of top recruiters worldwide considered employer branding essential to attracting and hiring the best talent. Another survey showed 75 percent of candidates were unwilling to accept offers from businesses with negative reputations.

The difference in employee turnover in companies with strong branding was 28 percent less than those with weak branding.[15] Wow!

So, what's the right way to reach a target audience, and how are companies effectively presenting their cultures and employee experiences? One successful trend is to understand and speak to different generations of job candidates.

While all humans share some fundamental needs, employers have identified preferences that are linked to age demographics. After all, today's workforce includes people born over a span of more than fifty years. From Boomers born after 1945 to Generation Z adults born before 2000, workers carry with them the cultural baggage common to their age brackets. Just as we all tend to prefer popular music from our youth, workers of various ages have differing expectations of their employers based on the predominant worldview of their prime. When we say, "the times, they are a-changing," this is what we mean.

So, what has changed from one generation to the next that is relevant to the workplace? According to "The New Meaning of Talent" survey:

- Communication styles
- Preferred management styles
- Preference to work on location or remotely
- Patience in time needed to secure promotions
- Prioritizing innovation of new ideas over stability of the status quo

---

[15] Human Capital Institute and Allegis Global Solutions, "Innovative Talent Acquisition Strategies," 3.

Managing a multi-demographic staff includes overcoming negative generational stereotypes and company culture biases held by individuals. Allegis Group's Tanya Axenson notes that the agile employer builds a workplace culture that transcends divisions by age groups and ideologies. She counsels business leaders to "bring all employees together through a common set of values."

This gives you ways to speak to the talent pool at large as well as distinct subsets of it. But there is another factor that will boost your readiness quotient: the ability to appeal to both active and passive job candidates. These could be classified as those with freshly remodeled résumés who are actively looking, and folks who are currently employed but open to opportunities, either now or down the road. They include workers who are:

> *A person's craft or skill is now more important than what the sign above the door says.*

- Unemployed
- Underemployed
- Disengaged
- Relocating
- Upwardly mobile

So, who is leading in developing their brand through culture and expressing that to the various candidate verticals? Companies that identify specific needs tend to do that well. Matt Charney, chief content officer of Allegis Global Solutions and executive editor of *Recruiting Daily,* described to me a particular acquisition problem that revealed its own solution—with a little help from an observant employee.

Charney was contracted for six weeks to help a major technology company create a world-class candidate experience. This wasn't an HR initiative; instead, it came from the CTO, as the company was experiencing an alarming downward spiral in terms of their offer acceptance ratio—a problem that they hadn't had during earlier stages of growth. Human Resources thought it was because compensation was below market or that the company had mixed reviews on Glassdoor; business stakeholders suggested the culprit was required relocation to Santa Barbara, one of the most expensive places to live in the United States, and in which this one enterprise was the only tech industry employer.

Research and surveying suggested that neither were correct. Candidates who declined offers cited primarily lack of fit, although few could articulate exactly what this meant. Charney and his team had to identify the problem before they could formulate a solution, but they'd hit a dead end.

Fortunately, a recruitment coordinator with about six months of experience overheard one of their meetings and had the courage to speak up. She was tasked with getting candidates from one site on campus to another and arranging their schedule and travel logistics; basically, administrative tasks. She revealed that she had many conversations as she drove candidates around, and a recurring theme was that they considered the company and job great, but that they didn't feel as if they "fit" in Santa Barbara. She further explained that while the process was focused on giving candidates a white-glove experience to sell the benefits of the company and role, there was no emphasis on selling the location.

When asked for a list of suggestions, she came up with several ideas that were quickly implemented: paying for spouses to fly out during the interview for a tour of the city, homes, and schools (plus a spa treatment by the beach!); adding interviews off-campus around the hot spots in the city; and, finally, ditching the chain hotel closest to the office for Airbnb stays during the interview process, so that a visit felt more like home and less like a work trip.

These were small changes that made a big difference—the company's accepted-offer ratio climbed by close to 50 percent within three months, and in follow-up surveys, no candidates identified "lack of fit" as the reason for declining their offers. With the average cost to interview one candidate at around $7,500, given the travel requirements, the improved acceptance rate was enormous. In one quarter, those small changes saved the company almost a million dollars in recruitment costs—all because one junior employee took the time to listen to candidates, identify their issues, and provide very simple solutions to what everyone had all assumed was a much more complex problem. From then on, coordinators were represented in every strategic TA meeting at the company and went from back-office support to strategic partners.

Creating more personal candidate experiences is one way to turn a somewhat negative or shaky aspect into a real draw. Consider where your company is weak in its EVPs and get some input from those know best to discover why. Then you can directly appeal to prospective talent on a personal level.

Partnerships to Manage the Platform

Most businesses spend less time and effort than they should—if any—in reviewing and upgrading their current processes. If your company does not revisit your strategic hiring and employee management plans, employer brand, and talent outreach efforts *at least annually,* you will not be able to successfully compete. Worse, your ability to meet your business goals will be severely hampered.

Or, suppose you do take these proactive steps, but your talent acquisition program is still falling short. If either of these scenarios are familiar to your organization, don't close this book yet. I know you're busy. Or you've got limited manpower. All you need is a little help integrating your work objectives with your branding and recruiting methods.

You'll find many books and consultants out there to help you improve general culture and marketing plans. Analyzing work processes and gaining visibility into the talent pipeline, however, require a specific and holistic approach. I recommend doing this in-house only if you can dedicate a team to researching, planning, and implementing a platform designed around your business objectives. Often, a third party can do this much more effectively. Let's look at the more focused help you can get by partnering with professionals that offer total talent solutions.

In considering potential partners, look for those that approach recruiting as "the best way to get the work done." If you've done your homework, you'll be clear on which projects will achieve your business goals, and which tasks must be performed to successfully complete projects. This positions you to pick and choose among your options in internal talent, contractors, online talent platforms, and automation.

A total talent platform partner will help you tie all the threads together. These professionals provide organizational analysis, brand refinement, talent searches, and candidate experience management designed toward your business objectives. This comprehensive strategy creates universal access to all forms of talent and enables selection based on the best way to get the work done. Hiring a recruitment process outsource (RPO) and a managed services provider (MSP) to support your current HR procedures will only get you part of the way. To pull off a makeover on this scale, you need the insight and planning power of work design architects, in addition to outsourcing specialists and recruitment managers, all working together. You'll want a partner firm that is rabid about gathering data regarding your organization's productivity, labor supply and demand, pay scales, etc.—and that can direct your team in how to use that information. Otherwise, you may suffer from "big data, little value" syndrome—having so much data in disparate systems that you are unable to analyze or apply it.

Yes, this is a huge undertaking, but well worth it in relation to the massive size of the prize. Achieving organizational readiness will literally spur a quantum leap over the competition for the talent your company wants and needs. At my firm, we measure this in many ways, but one simple indicator is time-to-hire. In companies using a total talent strategy, we've seen a drop in recruitment time by as much as 60 percent, which translates directly to money saved and productivity gained. So, be sure you select a partner that understands your talent history and that can project your future needs. This will form a well-rounded view of what you're doing right, what needs to change, and how to do it. There is no better way to reach an optimum agile state.

Several specific areas of activity will support your platform and create a sustainable framework that is open to revision as circumstances change. Here are some of the ways your organization can get started:

1. Evaluate and update your past models for matching workers to work.

Traditionally, employers fill open positions with the same type of worker who just walked out the door. This means automatically putting full-time employees or temporary contractors in the same slots. It may take someone outside your organization to drill down and ask the tough questions about what the work actually needs, and which workers are available to vie for the job.

For instance, it may make sense to bring a longtime contractor who has become familiar with your company in as a full-time employee. A working knowledge of your culture and business goals may put this individual far ahead of the learning curve that a new hire would face. On the other hand, filling a full-time position that has become more complex over time with just one person could be extremely limiting. A team of two or more contractors might provide a broader skill set with which to tackle more intricate projects.

The work design architects on your partnering team will have the vision and expertise to take your stakeholders through the question-and-answer process to develop the best talent model for the moment.

2. Project and prepare for future skills needs.

But what about tomorrow? Agility demands that we be ready for what is to come in both our business needs and the shifting talent marketplace. You need to set yourselves up to foresee contingencies and plan to meet them; a third party may be best able to do this dispassionately. Either way, use analytics to make reasonable projections that will let you prioritize departmental funding or seek talent exchange programs with leading companies in another field. This puts you in front of the other guys who are just noticing a void in their technology or talent pipeline when it is already too late to fill it.

3. Facilitate informed decisions about pay scales.

Simply offering what you've paid in the past or adjusting a salary for inflation after a vacancy is not a precise way to handle pay scales. Today's market rate may be affected by any number of factors beyond your company's past history. Offer too little and you'll attract less qualified candidates. This can happen when your team is not aware of a growing demand for certain skills or a shifting supply of trained applicants. Offer too much and you may wind up with overqualified and unsatisfied workers, or simply throw away money that could have been better spent. Letting professionals who track prevailing salaries guide your pay scale can help you make equitable and informed decisions about what work is worth in your locale and in the current remote market.

4. Identify and deliver a clear promise to the talent pool.

Recruiting today's Talentsumers requires a vigorous marketing strategy and people-centric employer value proposition. The new talent is thinking less about whether they can meet your criteria and more about whether you can meet theirs. Your EVP must speak directly to their *why* by defining what you have to offer first and what you're asking for much more subtly than you may have done in the past.   Your talent partners (internal talent acquisition function or an external partner) will help you hone this message and get it in front of the right eyes via a growing number of digital channels. These folks need to know how to make this part of an ongoing conversation by inviting feedback and engaging both active and passive prospective candidates, professional guilds, and training institutions. They need to compile data on media channels, user conversion, and the company's return on investment, in order to shape successful hiring policies over time.

5. Revise hiring processes to enhance the candidate experience.

Finally, talent professionals can help you upgrade your application process to make it as attractive as possible. Looking for jobs and sitting for interviews takes a lot of time and effort, and it's stressful. Why not make the process as easy as possible, and even enjoyable?

Talentsumers appreciate a streamlined application process. Online forms that autofill from a résumé, for example, save candidates time in resubmitting information that you already have. Are there other steps or requirements that can be eliminated? Do you really need to know where an applicant went to grade school? Talentsumers also expect quick responses. Even an automated "We've accepted your application" email and an initial personal reply within twenty-four hours is better than allowing candidates to wonder. A human interaction, of course, will leave a much better impression. If another employer connects faster, candidates may move on right away.

Your talent partners should help you develop ways to swiftly acknowledge and analyze applications, gauge suitability, and schedule your next hiring move. Being clued in to your company culture, EVPs, and AVPs, they will find opportunities to embed these things in each step of the application process and give candidates visibility into what it's like to work with you. Like consumers considering where to spend their money, workers want to be able to make informed choices about where or with whom to spend their lives.

Treating applicants with respect and appealing to their preferences reverberates beyond the individual encounter. This is how we create talent ambassadors. By keeping every contact positive, your company is more likely to be remembered well when candidates consider making referrals or future employment associations. Managers and HR staff can get caught up in details and lose sight of the overall experience on the other side of the desk. A vigilant partner can monitor and influence how candidates perceive the process.

Doug Bugie, Head of Global Franchise Expansion, Next Wave – FPC Worldwide

A few years ago, my organization at the time was tasked with finding people who were more customer services focused and less arrogant about 'locking in' customers to their company, telling them to take a hike if they had any complaints or issues. It was like having the right to sell one brand of beer once everyone was inside the sports stadium, if you don't like it, tough!

One of the leaders of the company likened this attitude to 'drive-by licensing'.

We were charged with changing the culture to engender to a more long-term customer centric kind of person. It took about 2 years for us to find and hire several hundred people of the right type to change their culture.

The interesting twist was there were about 30,000 applicants yearly to fill 500 jobs. We were instructed, quite wisely I thought, to make sure every applicant was treated personally and well vs automated email response. That way their 'rejection' didn't metastasize into anti-company sentiment. Every candidate was seen a potential customer or competitor who would be given a deep chip on their shoulder.

It became a great example of how caring about employer branding deeply, can also achieve a very pragmatic, long-term commercial result.

Part Three
GET READY!
Tactical Action for Strategic Value

Strategic Tool: Setting Priorities for Your Business

As you get into this section, you'll see there are a number of initiatives that I am recommending you crack on with. Yet, I know that every company is different and, therefore, so are their needs and priorities. To help you work in sync with yours, I'll share with you a tested model that I've used over the years with great success that I've dubbed, **Value vs. Complexity.** This is a framework used to manage risk and avoid failure in choosing which projects or strategies to do when. It is not my IP and is better known as Impact vs. Complexity. But, in the context of work and workforce design and transformation, I like to emphasize the ROI by calling it Value vs. Complexity.

Here's how it works. Each idea/plan/feature you are considering holds some business value in the form of potential improvements to your organization and payoffs for your customers, internal or external. Each also has some level of complexity. To set priorities for what to do first and later on, you can make a graph that plots each factor on an X/Y axis via a score of 1, 2, or 3 to indicate the impact of each particular element. I compile complexity and value scores using multiple measures for each, weighted by degree of importance. For example:

Value Score: High = 3, Medium = 2, Low = 1
Example Criteria:

Impact on Internal Efficiency	Compliance
	Visibility
Stakeholder Experience	Supplier Management
	ROI
Drives Quality	Cost Savings

Other criteria might be: alignment with strategic direction of organization; potential to increase reputation, agility, or competitive advantage; ability to open new markets, etc. You'll know what's of the most value to your organization.

Complexity Score: High = 3, Medium = 2, Low = 1
Example Criteria:

Technology Integrations Required	Geographic Spread
Resources	Change Management
Time to Go Live	Cost of Implementation
	Level of Process to Get Sign-Off

First, work up your scores based on the criteria you've selected. You'll wind up with totals (averages) between 1 and 3 for each initiative.

INITIATIVES	VALUE								COMPLEXITY							
	STAKEHOLDER EXPERIENCE	DRIVES QUALITY	COMPLIANCE	VISIBILITY	SUPPLIER ENGAGEMENT	HIGH ROI	COST SAVINGS	TOTAL (AVE)	LOW TECHNOLOGY INTEGRATIONS	LOW DEMAND FOR RESOURCES	SHORT TIME TO IMPLEMENT	LIMITED LOCATIONS	LIMITED CHANGE MANAGEMENT	LOW COST TO IMPLEMENT	LIMITED NEED FOR BUSINESS PLAN	TOTAL (AVE)
1 TECH BUILD	2	2	2	2	2	1	1	1.7	1	1	2	2	2	2	2	1.7
2 PROCESS DESIGN	2	2	2	1	1	2	1	1.6	1	3	2	3	3	2	2	2.3
3 SUPPLY CHAIN RFP	2	3	1	2	3	2	2	2.1	2	2	2	1	1	1	1	1.4
4 SOW REFRESH	2	3	3	3	3	1	1	2.3	1	2	3	2	2	2	1	1.9
5 AVP CREATION	3	3	3	3	2	3	3	2.9	3	3	3	3	3	3	3	3
6 VALUE MESSAGING	3	3	2	3	3	3	3	2.9	3	2	2	3	2	3	2	2.4

Then, plot the numbers on an X/Y graph, as in the following example:

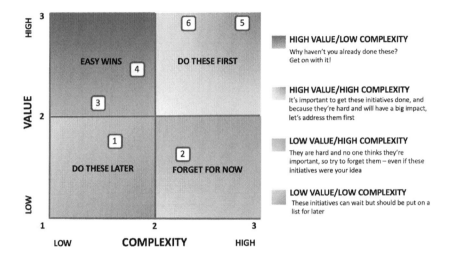

Finally, interpret each quadrant to arrive at your priorities:

1. **High Complexity/High Value:** These big-bang initiatives should be tackled first because they're difficult but will have a great impact.

2. **Low Complexity/High Value:** These look like sure winners. Why haven't you already done them? Get on with it!

3. **Low Complexity/Low Value:** Put these less-pressing initiatives on a list to get to later.

4. **High Complexity/Low Value:** These items are hard, and no one thinks they're important. So, try to forget them, for now—even if these initiatives were your idea!

CHAPTER 7

Prepare the Work for Workers

Action steps:

1. Deconstruct assignments
2. Map performance
3. Define roles and goals
4. Evaluate talent pipeline
5. Streamline work processes
6. Create a maintenance schedule

When you begin your mission to deconstruct your organization's work processes, keep your eye on the prize. What is it you want the organization—and in turn, your people—to accomplish? This should become your mantra throughout your readiness initiative. For each task, ask what you want the outcome to be. Start with the task, not the job description.

Let's take a very simple example. Your receptionist's job description may be to welcome customers, make sure everyone's ID is checked, answer the phone, and connect them with people who can give them desired information. Having defined that, you can now think about what the best outcome of those tasks might be. Would this role best be looked at as "head of visitor experience"? If so, how would the tasks be allocated, and what increased responsibility might we include in a newly defined role? Would it make sense to outsource security to a specialist firm so that the head of visitor experience can spend more time doing just that—giving visitors an enhanced experience? Perhaps that person could be redesigning the lobby or rethinking the auto-direct phone system. Once you look though a different lens, the ideas will start to flow.

Remember to include the actual performers in any discussion of how you shape the work. You might leave it up to them on a case-by-case basis. You might collaborate on new policies. Whatever you do, do not take away the tools they rely on before finding acceptable substitutes. Remember what happened when Initech took away Milton's favorite stapler in *Office Space?* He burned the place to the ground! When you get down to the nuts and bolts of what makes work work, ask the folks who are doing it what improvement looks like. Never stop asking, "How easy do we make it for you to do great work?"

Six Steps Toward Better Work Design

1. Deconstruct projects and assignments to their basic tasks.
First, go department by department and list the major functions they perform. In Human Resources, for instance, major functions include talent acquisition and employee management. You can then use the model laid out below to evaluate and revamp your workflows:

A WORK DESIGN ARCHITECTURE MODEL

This is a methodology I created to help understand and design the best way to get work done in any company. It will help you and your leadership team connect your organization's business objectives to its work architecture. I suggest using it to simplify the lexicon for how the company gets work done and to prepare yourselves for giving strategic advice to stakeholders.

A. Using the diagram as a template, begin with one business line or function. Start with **"Work,"** the column on the far right—it may sound counterintuitive, but bear with me—and ask:

- *What are the basic elements or operations needed to achieve successful work outcomes?*

List each step of the work that needs to be performed in order for that business line or function to be successful. Consider this a **list of tasks, not responsibilities.** For example, if a sales function, write, "Sell XYZ," not, "We are on the hook for sales" or "We have a salesforce that needs managing…."

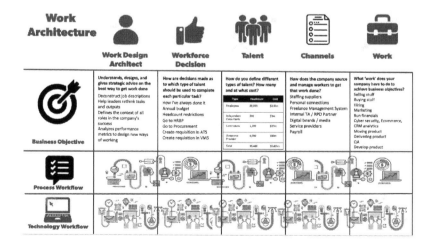

B. Once you have that list, pick one task at a time and work your way left. Consider your **"Channels"**:

- *How does the company currently source and manage workers to get that specific work done?*
  For example: *Staffing Suppliers, Personal Connections, Freelance Management Systems, Online Platforms, Internal Talent Acquisition, RPO Partner, Digital Boards, Social Media, Service Providers, Outsourced, Payroll Provider, etc.*

C. Then, think about the **"Talent"** you source or manage via each channel:

- *Which different types of talent do we use? How many and at what cost?*
  For example; *Employees, Independent Consultants, Contractors, Outsourced Providers, etc.*

D. Examine your **"Workforce Decision"** process:

- *Which criteria influence decisions about which type of talent should be used to complete each particular task? Should they be changed?*
  For example: *How I've Always Done It, Annual Budget, Headcount Restrictions, Go to HRBP, Go to Procurement, Create Requisition in Applicant Tracking System, Create Requisition in Vendor Management System*

E. Determine who has the qualifications, or who can be trained, to act as your **"Work Design Architect"**:

- *Who can be tasked with putting all of the above information together to best match our work process to workers, with our business goals in mind?*
  For example, who has the ability to: Deconstruct Job Descriptions, Help Managers and Leaders Rethink Tasks and Outputs, Define the Context That All Roles Play in Company's Success, Analyze Performance Metrics to Design New Ways of Working

F. Next, complete the bottom two rows—**"Process Workflow"** and **"Technology Workflow"**—by laying out the different processes and technology touch points or enablers for each type of talent or channel—whichever most makes the most sense for your circumstances.

G. Now that you have worked from right to left for a number of work tasks, complete **"Business Objectives."** For each of your major business objectives, work the table from left to right, considering what role you need the work design architect to play in the decision-making process. Ask:

- *Is there a different way to sell XYZ? Is there a better way to get *** done?*
- *Why do we use contractors for ***?*
- *Why do we outsource that element of the task?*
- *Is that the most effective and efficient way to get *** done?*

- *What talent and work architecture are we going to need for an upcoming new objective/business opportunity?*
- *(Add a stack of questions that are relevant to your business.)*

This model may appear simple as you review it here, but in practice it gets pretty complex and strategically, it is crucial. After all, who in your organization is asking these questions right now? Without that information at hand, you have not yet achieved readiness!

2. Map the performance of current talent/work matches.

Next, you'll want to analyze those segmented job summaries. The goal of this evaluation will be to understand how efficient and effective current hiring decisions are and to see where improvements can be made to better match the work to workers. This is particularly important when considering which tasks can be automated. Ask:

- *What is the task being performed?*
- *How is the work being done?*
- *Who is doing the work now? And how well?*
- *What technology is being used?*
- *What part of the process works well?*
- *What part needs improvement?*

Use anecdotal evidence and any performance data you've collected. If you haven't gotten that far, start with employee and manager surveys, and identify key performance indicators. Then, track those metrics and analyze them.

3. Define how each job role meets overall business goals. This will require a cross-departmental conversation, with the outcome directed at HR and Procurement. Linking positions or assignments to larger objectives reveals how individual actions come together to achieve them. This also shows which job skills produce which results. With that information, those who are doing the hiring can seek competencies, rather than rely on academic degrees and x number of years of experience.

Say you're looking for a website developer, and you've identified the major skills the job entails. If you find someone with demonstrated ability in programming, database administration, and content management, it might not matter which particular industry employed that person in the past. Such skills are transferrable to other sectors. In the same manner, a receptionist who served patients well in a doctor's office will probably be able to handle clients or customers in any field.

Looking at objectives is the precursor to deconstructing how work is performed in your company. It will allow you to hire based on abilities instead of a certain type of person, whether that's "college graduate," "doctor's office receptionist," or "nationally recognized expert." To some degree, breaking down the work into its basic parts will also deconstruct the potential worker to his or her relevant skill set. Good to know!

Now you're getting some visibility into how well your stated job requirements help you achieve (or not achieve) your end goals. It may be time to adjust those expectations, especially when it comes to hiring status. A temporary contractor might more swiftly handle a project that was assigned to a full-time worker over a longer period of time, due to the latter's remaining workload.

4. Streamline and improve work processes. By now, you have surveyed or had informal talks with your employees about how work works—and where it doesn't work quite so well. Rely on them to suggest which tasks are redundant, less efficient, or a pain in the neck. Then huddle with project leaders and managers to redefine workflows. Here, you'll see real performance shifts. If you've made the right changes, productivity will improve. If not, you'll see where a new approach is necessary.

This is a win-win effort for everyone. You'll continually reshape your work methods toward improvement, and at the same time, make work easier or more enjoyable for employees. Continue to ask for feedback on that count. Generally, when we tailor workflows to satisfy both workers and end goals, we'll hit upon the best way to get the job done.

One avenue is to increase the use of RPA technology to streamline processes. Incorporate best practices in scheduling and meetings by using online and mobile communications technology. This opens the door to remote teams, global talent access, and virtual collaboration that saves time and money. Digitizing administrative work, such as submitting expense reports and contractor invoices, reduces time-consuming manual tasks and frees workers to concentrate on other priorities.

Give employees access to the information they need in order to eliminate search time or multiple phone calls. An online database or file sharing system accessed via desktop or mobile device can save man-hours while giving your people the tools they need to do superior work at their fingertips. Sometimes, just the ability to answer important questions quickly keeps the work process flowing and employees free of frustration.

Older workers or anyone less technically inclined, however, may see new automated systems as obstacles instead of improvements. As you upgrade technologically, be sure to provide walk-throughs or more in-depth training to those who need it. Again, you'll more swiftly increase productivity while reducing the aggravation caused by trial-and-error learning.

Robotic Process Automation: Guy Kirkwood, Chief Evangelist, UiPath

A great example of creating competitive advantage through improved employee engagement came to us from Karl Nolan, Chief Executive of Generali Link. He reported that, since implementing RPA from UiPath, "the mood music of our organisation has changed, we have happier employees, and we now measure our service in terms of compliments rather than complaints." As automation in the workplace potentially moves to the point where there is a robot for every person, this type of culture change will become more prevalent.

---

5. Evaluate your talent pipeline for its ability to achieve your goals. Your readiness work is beginning to pay off in transparency alone. The next chapter will help you map your talent "holdings" by skill set, and having enumerated which skills are needed to complete the steps toward your business goals, you can answer this crucial question as often as you need to: Do we have the talent to achieve that?

As you become more accurate in determining your talent readiness, you'll also be able to project whether your current or accessible talent will be able to meet your future needs. This is a discussion you'll return to often. You're entering a new era in which available talent and business goals will become inseparable.

6. Create a maintenance schedule for reevaluation. After completing a comprehensive workflow redesign, it's tempting to dust off your hands and consider it done. Those days are gone! As your final task, build reevaluation into your annual or biannual schedule. You've already been through the process and know what has to be done. All you have to do is resolve to do that again—but do it *as if for the first time*. Preconceived ideas will inhibit the gains you can make.

By keeping your finger on the pulse of your workflows, you'll always know where you stand in your talent supply and demand. If you can't answer whether your talent architecture is sufficient to achieve a particular goal, you need to take another look at how the work is getting done. Likewise, to successfully compete for talent with the high-demand skills to achieve desired outcomes, organizations must keep their process options open. Periodically examining work processes with a completely open mind will help your company reach this state of agility.

CHAPTER 8

Prepare Your Talent Pipeline

Action steps:

1. Get stakeholders on board
2. Review talent needs
3. Investigate automated and unsalaried options
4. Prepare outreach to every talent channel
5. Network to build talent alliances
6. Adjust policies

B y now, you're aware of the talent stakes and clued in to what is working for successful companies in the new landscape. Set aside some time and assemble your crew. You're ready to map out your own plan for achieving talent readiness. You'll want to go about this with the laser focus of a heist team in a Quentin Tarantino movie—and dial it up a notch. After all, look what happened to everyone but "Mr. Pink" (Steve Buscemi) in *Reservoir Dogs*. (Yep. All dead.)

Since you can never be too well prepared, it's still useful to learn about which directions to take. The steps listed above offer one path toward understanding where your organization stands in relation to talent readiness. Let this serve as a template from which to begin plotting your entry into the new talent pipeline.

Six Ways to Reach Talent Readiness

1. Get stakeholders on board for new talent pursuits. If your company has not yet shifted to the view that all types of hiring are on the table, this will be your first order of business. The goal is simply opening people's minds to routes that haven't been tried before. As The Heritage Group learned, we vastly increase our talent pools when we move beyond the last thing we did to fill each role in the work chain. The immediate obstacle is encouraging different departments—HR, Procurement, IT, Legal, Risk, etc.—to function together on talent.

If this seems like a superfluous task, remember the six Ps: the old saying that *prior planning prevents piss-poor performance.* Or, as Liz Huldin of THG more politely puts it, the "go slow to go fast" approach is an effective plan for comprehensive action. She sees the first move in a change initiative as building trust. With buy-in from the whole team, each faction is ready and willing to move forward as one.

In any change scenario, a lack of understanding on rationale and contingencies tends to produce resistance. Color in those fuzzy outlines, and people are more accepting and trusting. The solution at

THG was not to tell people what management thought they needed to know, however, but to ask. Surveying employees about their values and priorities, in addition to the changes at hand, provided a clear picture of where opposition might arise. Then, the company was able to address those issues before objections were raised. The survey responses also indicated ways in which workers already were independent and innovative, so an appeal to their existing agility could be made.

Huldin says this deliberate approach was worth the time and effort. The organization prepared people to accept change as a concept first, and the specific changes in their talent program second. "The result," she says, "is a culture that moves quickly to embrace new changes, whether using a new technology or implementing a program across multiple operating companies. The slow process of building trust upfront leads to speed and agility in the execution of the strategy."

How will your enterprise go about this? Start at the top! Business leaders must own the need to revisit hiring practices and the state of the workforce on a recurring basis. The influx of automation requires attention right now—it's too pervasive an issue to delegate to IT or HR alone. If top executives understand the technology and its consequences, they can guide other team members to help the company adapt. They can start a conversation with employees to prepare them for change. If human-staffed positions are to be lost to greater efficiency,

Who are the kingmakers in the company—those connectors, influencers, and disruptors who do whatever it takes to get s**t done? These are your champions of change.

they can protect people with new skills training and help them move to different jobs.

We simply do not have the luxury of sticking with one game plan any longer. Get the ball rolling with buy-in. All you have to do is present this as a life-or-death means of staying competitive. If that doesn't make the choice easy enough, you can always play that last scene from *Reservoir Dogs* for your team at the meeting.

2. Review past, present, and future talent needs.

To both convince the undecided and make informed decisions, you'll want the numbers on this. But chances are you might not have that data. Remember, a large chunk of HR leaders surveyed in 2018 claimed to be flying blind when it came to making their next hiring choices:

- 30 percent said total talent demand was not tracked across their organization
- 29 percent said total talent supply was not visible
- 34 percent had no system for measuring talent acquisition performance

Determine whether your company has the data to understand: a) where you have unfilled talent needs; b) what your current talent supply looks like; and c) what your success and failure rates are in recruitment metrics. Without this kind of visibility, your entire organizational agility can be held back by long hiring cycles, high payroll expenses, and quality issues due to poor matches or unfilled positions.

Get this information! Collect it all in one place, so that you can make educated decisions about where you source talent, how much you pay them, and how well you engage them. Knowing what works and what doesn't is critical. Include a means for querying process departments about what type of skills they might need in the future.

Then, hold a briefing that lays out this history in your company. Plot where you were (your old hiring models) and where you are now. Decide where you want to be in one, two, or three years' time. Then you'll know how far you need to travel.

3. Investigate automated and unsalaried help options. I distinguish these as a separate category of talent because they are, thus far, largely underestimated or untapped. As capital-saving alternatives to full-time employees, they can't be beat. Initial investment in artificial intelligence and automated processes, if they are judiciously implemented, will pay for itself. Additionally, unpaid human workers who are attracted for reasons other than monetary ones represent a loyal workforce that might be evergreen. You certainly don't want to miss out on an opportunity like that.

Again, return to fact gathering. After documenting your work processes and reducing them to their basic parts, your team will be able to see which steps are efficient, which are not, and whether they are cost-effective. Then you can ask whether automation would be an improvement. For instance, accounting reconciliations that could be performed digitally would free human employees to do less repetitive parts of the job. Rather than simply replacing workers, this lets them put their more intuitive skills toward analysis or other high-value tasks. It also creates a need for new positions that coordinate machine-based work, alerting recruiters to search for that type of talent in advance.

4. Prepare outreach to every talent channel. Is there a demographic you haven't considered in your talent outreach? Maybe your enterprise is one that naturally attracts people in a group you serve. This could be military veterans, teachers, or retirees. Folks who are transitioning out of jobs or retiring may still want to put their skills to good use. Consider which roles in your company might be attractive to people in these groups. Flag positions for which experienced people from related sectors would be most productive and include this outreach in your brand messaging.

Another underused hiring strategy is an appeal to qualified workers with disabilities. You can get all kinds of help in this area, from government pay subsidies to recruiting services aimed specifically at the disabled. It may be worth hiring a consultant or a talent solutions firm, such as Gettinghired.com, to perform an audit of your skills needs, work processes, and workplace accessibility. You might also find free help with these tasks through advocacy groups such as Job Accommodation Network, Wayfinder Family Services, or National Industries for the Blind.

If you decide that's a go, your HR department can turn to supporting organizations to raise awareness for your company at job fairs and conferences, while simultaneously promoting your employer brand. Consider contributing to or partnering with:

- **Getting Hired**
  www.gettinghired.com
- **The Arc**

www.thearc.org

- **Autism Speaks**
  www.autismspeaks.org
- **The Epilepsy Foundation**
  www.epilipsy.com
- **Wounded Warrior Project**
  www.woundedwarriorproject.com
- **National Multiple Sclerosis Society**
  www.nationalmssociety.org

Adding disabled workers to your diversity statements shows that your company is prepared to hire and welcome those with disabilities. GettingHired puts it well: it's important for organizations to recognize that diversity in hiring does not simply mean a focus on gender and ethnicity. Connecting skilled professionals to inclusive employers and advocacy organizations in the private and nonprofit sectors gives employers direct access to the undertapped labor pool of people with disabilities.

How about other in-need segments of the workforce? One energy services corporation attracts seniors who have not been employed for two or more years by offering "returnships." These three-month, paid gigs give older workers fresh experience as well as coaching and training to make them viable job candidates once more. Organizations such as The Mom Project specialize in creating opportunities for mums to re-skill and reenter the workforce into roles with companies that understand and support working motherhood.

Now, think about where your team is still not open-minded enough. Would they hire a creative type to help educate staff on a new IT program? How about adding a numbers geek to customer service ranks? As we rethink hiring people in relation to actual work goals, résumés and past experience may not tell the whole story. Often a new perspective is just what's needed in a role to foster innovation and efficiency. As we discussed in the last chapter, opening up job requirements beyond the rote descriptions we've relied on in the past brings in valuable people we would not have considered before. Goals, roles, and skill requirements are changing so swiftly that the person we hire today might be obsolete by tomorrow ... unless we screen for learning competency over finite experience.

Sometimes Naiveté Can Be a Great Thing

Once upon a time, when working with companies that were passionate about tapping onto their Gen Y workforce for ideas, we used a "mirror board" model for brainstorming and identifying the fast-track superstars. Each time the Board of Directors sat, the younger cohort—or mirror board—would receive the same agenda, with any sensitive or confidential subject matter redacted. Both groups would meet separately, and then come together to debrief later and share conversations and decisions, etc. (I always got a kick out of the debrief sessions, as most of the time the "real" Board would say, "You go first!"— in case the other guys had better ideas, I guess!)

We used this model with a retail bank that was looking to open a number of branches across China in an aggressive time frame: thirty branches in the next three years. Given the regulatory hoops, that plan was quite a stretch. Well, the mirror board presented a plan to the company Board to open all thirty in one year. As crazy-ambitious as that was, a few of the youngsters were invited to be part of the project, and one year later they had opened twenty-five new branches.

At a meeting to review the success of the mirror-board initiative and the lessons learned, I approached the branch expansion team and asked; "How on Earth did you come close to your goal of thirty openings in a year?" The response was magical: "We didn't know it was supposed to take all three years. We seriously didn't know any better!"

The growth of new fields and the push of technology are encouraging more companies to favor potential over experience. In fact, 47 percent of HR executives surveyed said they no longer require applicants to meet a certain number of years of experience within a particular job field to be considered for a position.[16] It's possible to understand how people think and learn, in order to project what they are capable of. Many HR departments issue personality tests as part of the application process. Besides personality and psychological assessments, factors such as problem-solving ability, a history of mentorship, and professional and educational achievements indicate areas of potential.

Assemble a workforce that is uniquely situated to get the work done, even when the demands of work change.

---

[16] Allegis Group, "The New Meaning of Talent," found that only 53 percent of hiring managers still use years of expertise as a part of a job requirement, 11.

And, who's to say that yesterday's experience will apply tomorrow? Demonstrating ability through work samples or problem scenarios shows what job candidates can do now. If a new demand arises based on a company's work goals, recruiters can determine if one of their current employees might be well suited to the task. This shows why one of the giants in the technology arena scrapped requirements for college degrees from job applicants. The company prefers to screen for learning style and capacity and provide their own training. This flips the old equation and assembles a workforce that is uniquely situated to get the work done, even when the demands of work change.

5. Network to build talent alliances with other companies. Trading or loaning employees between like-minded business eliminates having to search from scratch for some skilled people. It also expands your roster of potential talent ambassadors, who can steer referrals your way. Brainstorm potential alliances with compatible companies for skill sets that your company lacks—such as tech firms, film and video production, or specialty markets you are looking to enter.

It's not out of the question to partner with competitors, either. When tech was still nascent, companies like Microsoft and Hewlett-Packard made friends of opponents Intel and Canon. They are stronger today for it.

6. Adjust employee policies to apply to all hiring statuses. The focus here is on "normalizing" contingent workers to include them in all of the usual interactions you have with your employees. For instance, if you're serious about putting all new hires on board with your company's culture and purpose, you should be using the same steps with contractors that you do with permanent employees. Maybe you walk them through your mission, values, and vision statements, as well as workplace rules and other technicalities. I hear you screaming "co-employment," but why marginalize contractors? You want them to feel part of the team and to follow protocol. If they work remotely, sharing and discussing company values become even more important as a bonding tactic and a way to encourage working in line with the rest of your staff. Proactively think through how you can operate within the parameters of what you can compliantly do, rather than using the "co-employment" flag as the tail that wags the dog!

If you improve the experience for contractors, you'll reduce your risk for misuse of sensitive information and increase the type of good will that creates talent ambassadors. Standardizing offboarding processes has a similar effect. You'll tighten up your access pool to limit unauthorized cyber activity, plus use the exit interview to gain valuable information. And your last contact with a temporary worker will provide closure, leaving both sides aware of future prospects. Even if you think you won't need that employee down the road, you just might. Meanwhile, you've left them with a good impression of your company to pass along to others.

CHAPTER 9

Prepare Your Brand Message

Action steps:

1. Identify company "story"
2. Get employee input
3. Take action in work design and cultuı
4. Define target-market EVPs and AVPs
5. Streamline job descriptions
6. Reach out to talent

A clear picture of your goals, the work methods to achieve them, and the people to do it all come together in your employer brand. This may mirror or be compatible with your consumer brand, but it must be articulated in a distinct manner. Having arrived at the most desirable path to achievement, you now know which type of employees can get you where you're going.

You understand the generational similarities and differences among the workforce and can speak to demographic sectors in the most direct way. You know what you want, and whom you want. That's readiness. Now, go out there and get them!

Six Actions to Connect with the Best People

1. Identify your side of the company "story." As you consider what your organization is famous for in the realm of employment, think about what you want your message to achieve. What does the candidate want to hear? Job descriptions for certain positions are theoretically the same for any company. Your company story is what will set you apart from the competition in publicizing job openings. What's unique is the experience of working for *you.*

If you were applying for a job at your company, why would you choose to work there?

First, you'll sketch out what company and HR leaders think that story is. Later, you'll get your staff's take on that. Things may look different from the other side of the desk. But describing what you think makes your company stand out will lay the groundwork for telling a true story. Ask: *What are our strong points in company culture? How do we live our stated values in doing the work that we do? How does our enterprise contribute to something larger than just the marketplace?*

Now, put these elements in perspective by thinking about what those things lend to the employee experience. How does having an open-door policy, for instance, affect both top-tier and low-level staff? How does your particular value system influence things that are important to workers on the job, such as teamwork and accountability? Try to project. If you were applying for a job at your company, why would you choose to work there? Answering questions about culture, work processes, and employee policies will provide the outline of a compelling narrative.

2. Get employee input on their experience. Next, find out how close your version is to what workers have to say. You can go about this formally or informally but be thorough and get a cross-section of feedback from your workforce. Here are a couple of options:

- Host roundtables on the topic. Read off the company line, and then invite staff to offer their opinions on how closely you've described their day-to-day working lives. Then discuss how the underlying values and culture contribute to that.

- Go the survey route once more. This can be as simple as a two-question email that asks how easy it is for people to do their assigned tasks and where improvements could be made. Or you can print your story as you perceive it, share it, and ask questions about how accurate that is to individuals' actual experiences.

- Review anonymous social media posts about your company written by workers on platforms such as Glassdoor and LinkedIn. Read between the lines to gauge what they have to say in light of what you think your company's strengths and weaknesses are.

You can even do all of these things, to cut through anticipated bias and inhibitions about conveying negative things that workers assume the company doesn't want to hear. Of course, you can use anonymous surveys. But, getting input from identified sources, as well, will help you home in on your target audiences for different jobs, which you'll need to know later in this process.

3. Take action in work design and culture. Now, eliminate the distance between the two overarching stories. This may take some dedication on the company's part to improving things thought to be top-notch or implementing new ideas gleaned from employee feedback. You just asked your workers what's most important to them in being employed, making a living, and doing their best work. If your company is falling short in any areas, shore them up.

Ask whether your organization's work design and prevailing culture satisfy the priorities of today's workers:

- Does your company offer flexible work arrangements? Many candidates base their employment choices on the ability to set their own schedules or work remotely. Part-time and work-sharing options are not passé.
- Have you given employees control over their careers? Training and advancement opportunities should be transferrable to relationships with other companies when yours has ended.
- Do you have technology-enabled perks? The ability to trade paperwork for online forms or to use video conferencing instead of mandatory in-person meetings is attractive to Talentsumers.

Of course, we want to paint a rosy picture of work life for prospective talent. Make sure reality lives up to that promise. Revisit any segments of your work processes that folks complain about. You don't have to cater to every whim, but a consensus will tell you if changes need to be made in order to live up to your brand message. Should feedback reveal low morale, a lack of trust, or a disconnect with the product of people's labor, take action to improve your culture. Often, better systems of communication, acknowledgement, and problem-solving will correct the inconsistencies that hamper engagement.

4. Define your target-market EVPs and AVPs. Your pipeline and process evaluations have shown you which sectors to tap for talent. Choose a few main groups to appeal to. Suppose you've determined that the ideal mix for your company currently includes 50 percent full-time employees, 25 percent freelance contractors, and 25 percent unpaid workers drawn from internships and a volunteer program. While all will share some of the same employment expectations, part of your message will need to be tailored to each group.

Use what you've learned from crafting your company story and reviewing what employees most appreciate from their work experience. Put yourself in the shoes of applicants from different demographics and those seeking different hiring relationships. For each group, how do your employee and assignment value propositions address the highly ranked desires for developmental opportunity, performance recognition, interactive management, and team collaboration? Those answers may illuminate

> *Candidates searching through job posts immediately click off when they feel they don't measure up to the 'must have' specifications listed.*

your EVPs and AVPs. These points of value will be used to inform your job postings and advertisements.

5. Streamline job descriptions. If you haven't already revamped your job descriptions by removing superfluous requirements, do it now with your open positions. Candidates searching through job posts immediately click off when they feel they don't measure up to the specifications listed. For instance, "must have experience in x, y, and z programs" knocks a lot of people out of the running. Decide where your company can rely on a candidate's track record or tested learning capacity instead of specific requirements. Suddenly, you've widened the field considerably.

When potential applicants read your ad on the company website or an online employment hub, they should learn more about the experience than the basic tasks you compiled during deconstruction. They want to know less about how many reports need to be filed and more about how easy and satisfying you make it for them to file those reports. They want to know how managing your databases or attending to your customers will prepare them for the next stage of their working lives—and that is no longer an unreasonable request.

Remember, it's a talent-driven market. Your job description can either be a first, or last, connection to prospects. As you compose job ads, keep in mind how the work satisfies the worker. You'll have plenty of opportunities to vet people's capabilities before making a commitment.

6. Reach out to all talent constituents. And now we've come to the core purpose of recruiting professionals: attracting talent. All of the prep work we've discussed bolsters what is essentially a marketing initiative. Telling your company story so that it presents your brand and EVPs in ways that will resonate with candidates may require more oomph than your current outreach plan has. Your talent platform team must become brand experts, social media experts, and technology masters. So! Train them for that.

Then, delegate the work of filling open positions and keeping a running conversation with passive candidates going. This work must seamlessly mesh with best marketing practices. Find out what hits the mark on a case-by-case basis. Use metrics like time-to-hire, applicant demographics, and questionnaires embedded in interviews or the onboarding process to determine how well your branding effort is working. Track the quality of candidates, the rate of successful hires, and any failed plans—such as a volunteer program that doesn't get off the ground—and change them.

Gathering data that makes connections between your branding message and recruiting performance will help you build a strong appeal to active job seekers and continually improve it. At the same time, you'll want to maintain contact with passive sources for future talent needs. This positions you to jump at new business opportunities without a big delay in looking for human resources.

Use your company website and social media posts to attract interest from the workforce at large. Post content that demonstrates your company's expertise in its field, as well as its views on employment culture and management. Use your EVPs and AVPs as touch points for your leadership on issues of high concern to workers. You can provide value for passive candidates by showing them paths to acquiring new skills or taking on new roles that they might not have considered yet. Welcome them by providing links to comment online or connect with your recruiters via the web page.

You may also reach out individually to candidates who express interest, or to institutions that might have pools of potential talent, such as universities or technical schools. Be consistent in your messaging across all of these channels, to strengthen and solidify your employer brand. The goal is to make your company indispensable to Talentsumers. Tell them why they wouldn't want to work anywhere else on Earth!

A FINAL WORD

Thanks for the chat! You can see that getting organizations to think differently and tap into the talent they have under their noses to achieve success is my soapbox, my passion, and my purpose. It ties into my reason for being attracted to the world of staffing in the first place: a happy accident showed me I could apply my gifts to new situations. Otherwise, I'd be speaking to a butcher's convention or letting my "handicap" keep me from playing golf right now.

So, let's keep the conversation going. I ask you to bring up these topics with your peers, your boss, and—most importantly—those who work for you. We have a saying that we live by across the Allegis Group: *Serve Down.* That's how we achieve engagement, encourage innovation, and realize business goals. Working for others enhances our purpose, and we have a great time doing it.

Still wondering how to broach the subject of change? Perhaps start by using these four, little words that put dread into most people, particularly men: "We need to talk." That's a text you don't want to get at work ... but it gets your attention! Once the shock wears off, the request can be seen for what it really is, a call for transparency and consensus.

Get your people together, preferably over pizza and beer, and discuss the ideas I've given you a glimpse into throughout this book. Try out some of the models for work and workforce redesign. Make 'change' in your organization be about learning, not about leaving things behind. After forty years, I certainly don't have all the answers, but I continue to learn every day. My golf game is a testament to that.

Now that you are hopefully more prepared to get the ball rolling, I'll leave you with what I believe to be the best definition of improvement, and that is, "making a change for the better." So, your call to action is be open to CHANGE and do something about it ... *NOW!*

–Bruce

P.S. I worked with a freelancer I hired on Upwork to help write this book and a book designer on Fiverr.com – truly living the new world of work!

Printed in Great Britain
by Amazon